Gertrude Strohm

The Universal Common Sense Cookery Book

Practical Recipes for Household Use

Gertrude Strohm

The Universal Common Sense Cookery Book
Practical Recipes for Household Use

ISBN/EAN: 9783744795210

Printed in Europe, USA, Canada, Australia, Japan

Cover: Foto ©Lupo / pixelio.de

More available books at **www.hansebooks.com**

THE UNIVERSAL Common Sense COOKERY BOOK

PRACTICAL RECIPES FOR HOUSEHOLD USE

BY THE FOLLOWING AUTHORITIES:

MRS. D. A. LINCOLN,
MISS M. PARLOA,
MARION HARLAND
MRS. WASHINGTON,
THOMAS J. MURREY
AND OTHERS

BOSTON:
CHARLES E. BROWN & CO.

PREFACE.

The compiler desires to express her sense of the large debt of gratitude she owes to the many authors and publishers whose generous contributions have enabled her to carry out a cherished plan. It is a pleasure to mention the names of those to whom she is so much indebted, and she desires to render her acknowledgments to the following: —

Mrs. Harriet Beecher Stowe, Mrs. A. D. T. Whitney, Mrs. H. P. Spofford, Mrs. R. H. Davis, Mrs. Mary Mapes Dodge, Marion Harland, Mrs. D. A. Lincoln, Mrs. Mary Stuart Smith, Miss Juliet Corson, and Miss Maria Parloa, Miss Estelle M. Hatch of the "Boston Globe," Mr. John Burroughs, and Mr. Charles D. Warner. Also to the Rev. John H. Thomas of Indiana, the holder of the copyright of the work published in Dayton, O.; Messrs. Houghton, Mifflin, & Co.; Estes & Lauriat; Roberts Brothers; Harper & Brothers; G. P. Putnam's Sons; Dick & Fitzgerald; Dodd, Mead, & Co.; J. B. Lippincott Co.; Mr. Charles J. Peterson; Belford, Clarke, & Co.; the publishers of "Arthur's Home Magazine" and "Godey's Lady's Book," of "Good Housekeeping," "The Caterer," and "The Cook."

Also to the many editors who have aided her, and whose papers will be found duly credited throughout this volume.

INDEX TO LITERARY SELECTIONS AND QUOTATIONS.

	PAGE
DINNER SCENE FROM "RIQUET À LA HOUPPE:" *Mrs. Anne Thackeray Ritchie*	3
QUOTATION FROM "THE BALLAD OF BOUILLABAISSE:" *Thackeray*	7
THE TROUT: *A. B. Street*	15
KISSES AT MARKET: *Anonymous*	29
BEEFSTEAK PUDDING. "MARTIN CHUZZLEWIT:" *Dickens*	32
MUTTON AND TURNIPS: *Charles Lamb*	38
ROAST PIG: *Charles Lamb*	43
BACON AND EGGS: *Father Prout's Relics*	45
THE SABBATH SUPPER CHIME: *Puck*	49
ON TRIPE. "THE CHIMES:" *Dickens*	50
SAM LAWSON'S TURKEY. "OLDTOWN FOLKS:" *Mrs. Stowe*	59
ROAST GOOSE. "A CHRISTMAS CAROL:" *Dickens*	65
STUFFED PEACOCK: *Pierre Blot*	67
PIGEON PIE. "THE SKETCH-BOOK:" *Irving*	71
ON GAME. "STEVEN LAWRENCE, YEOMAN:" *Mrs. Annie Edwards*	75
THE 'POSSUM: *Arkansaw Traveller*	77
"TOSS US UP AN OMELET." "THE MAID OF CROISSEY:" *Mrs. Gore*	83
QUOTATION FROM ESSAYS: *R. W. Emerson*	87
DESCRIPTION OF DAIRY. "ADAM BEDE:" *George Eliot*	89
THE MUSHROOM: *Campbell*	93
ASPARAGUS: *Charles Lamb*	96
THE MAIZE. "HIAWATHA:" *H. W. Longfellow*	97
CABBAGE. "MY SUMMER IN A GARDEN:" *C. D. Warner*	103
THE ONION. "MY SUMMER IN A GARDEN:" *C. D. Warner*	105
CELERY: *John Burroughs*	106

INDEX TO SELECTIONS.

	PAGE
EXTRACT FROM "AUNT CINDY'S DINNER:" *Sarah Winter Kellogg*	137
SCENE FROM "MARY POWELL:" *Mrs. Manning*	146
QUOTATION FROM "LOCUSTS AND WILD HONEY:" *Burroughs*	147
SCENE FROM "MARGARET:" *Sylvester Judd*	155
SCENE FROM "MARGRET HOWTH:" *Mrs. R. H. Davis*	157
FRUMENTY. "ESSAYS OF ELIA:" *Lamb*	160
AN APPLE PUDDING. "WE GIRLS:" *Mrs. Whitney*	163
APPLE DUMPLINGS: *Charles Lamb*	196
STRAWBERRIES: *Dr. Boteler and John Burroughs*	171
BLACKBERRIES: *Charles Mackay*	172
PUMPKIN PIE. "THE PUMPKIN:" *J. G. Whittier*	182
MINCE PIE. "LEGEND OF SLEEPY HOLLOW:" *Irving*	186
THE PARTY. "DONALD AND DOROTHY:" *Mrs. Dodge*	191
JESSIE'S BARGAINS: *Mrs. H. P. Spofford*	215
SCENE FROM "MY PRECIOUS BETSY:" *Morton*	223
POEM ON HERBS: *Shenstone*	231
QUOTATION FROM "THE CULPRIT FAY:" *J. R. Drake*	233

CHAPTER I.

SOUPS.

UNIVERSAL COOKERY BOOK.

SOUPS.

"WHERE *is* Sylvia?" cried Colonel King, in a harsh voice. His back was turned to the window. "Sophy, why didn't you look after her?"

"There she is!" cried Frank Lubworth. "What can she be doing in the garden?" And, in answer to an imploring look of Mrs. King's, he added, "I will go after her: don't you wait." ...

"It makes her father so nervous," said Mrs. King plaintively, raising her voice. "I can't think what to do. It is just like her to go for a walk in the garden, when we are all waiting dinner. Now, Sophy never keeps us."

"Don't apologize," said the old lady. "Sylvia is quite pretty enough to keep us all waiting, and Sophy, who isn't pretty, is punctual; so it is all as it should be. Clear soup?" "Yes."

"My poor Sophy!" said the mother, who always seemed to take a melancholy view of every thing. "It seems so hard that Sylvia should have all the beauty of the family.—(No soup?) I can't take soup: it is a great privation to me.—Aunt Dormer! If you, with all your experience, could suggest any means by which we could give her a little of her sisters' good sense and thoughtfulness"—

"Suggest?" said the old lady, peppering her soup, "don't ask me to suggest. Find her a good husband, my dear: a punctual man, who can remind her when dinner is ready. Let him have a little money to pay for it too."—RIQUET À LA HOUPPE: *Mrs. Anne Thackeray Ritchie.*

Brown Stock.

"Take one pound of lean beef, shin, leg, ox-cheek, or from the clod; cut in slices, and place at the bottom of a greased saucepan, adding a little water to prevent its burning. Add a piece of lean bacon, cut in slices: a more or less quantity is immaterial,—from one-quarter to nearly the same amount of beef. Cover close to draw out the gravy gently, and then allow it nearly to dry until it becomes brown, then pour in sufficient boiling water to entirely cover the meat, skimming it frequently, and putting in salt, whole peppers, pot-herbs, and vegetables of any kind. After boiling gently for five or six hours, pour the broth from the meat, and let it stand during the night to cool. (Soup should never be suffered to stand in any vessel of tin, copper, or iron, to get cold.) In the morning take off the scum and fat, heat it, and put it away in a stone jar for future use. This will form a foundation for all the best brown soups."

Veal Stock.

Chop up three slices of bacon and two pounds of the neck of veal; place in a stewpan with a pint of water or beef-stock, and simmer for half an hour; then add two quarts of stock, one onion, a carrot, a bouquet of herbs, four stalks of celery, half a teaspoonful of bruised whole peppers, and a pinch of nutmeg with a teaspoonful of salt; boil gently for two hours, removing the scum in the mean time. Strain into an earthen crock, and when cold remove the fat. A few bones of poultry added, with an additional quantity of water or stock, will improve it. — FIFTY SOUPS: *Thomas J. Murrey. White, Stokes, & Allen, Pubs.*

Bouillon.

Four pounds of beef from the middle of the round, two pounds bone, two quarts cold water, one tablespoonful salt, four peppercorns, four cloves, one tablespoonful mixed herbs. Wipe and cut the meat and bones into small pieces; add the water, and heat slowly; add the seasoning, and simmer five hours. Boil down to three pints; strain, remove the fat, and season with salt and pepper. Serve in cups at luncheons, evening companies, etc. Boil one onion, half a carrot, and half a turnip, with it if you like. — THE BOSTON COOK-BOOK: *Mrs. D. A. Lincoln. Roberts Brothers, Pubs.* (*By per.*)

Pot-au-Feu.

Put in a saucepan six pounds of beef (bones included), cut into two or three pieces; three-quarters of a pound of mixed vegetables, such as onions, carrots, turnips, leeks, white cabbage, and celery with its leaves left on, all cut in good-sized pieces; three small spoonfuls of salt, one of pepper, and one of sugar; add eight pints of water; let it boil gently three hours; remove the fat; add crusts of roll or slices of bread, either previously toasted or plain, and serve. — DAINTY DISHES: *Lady Harriet St. Clair.*

Rabbit Soup.

Cut one or two rabbits into joints; lay them for an hour in cold water; dry and fry them in butter till about half done, with four or five onions and a middling-sized head of celery, cut small; add to this three quarts of cold water, one pound of split peas, some pepper and salt; let it stew gently for four or five hours, then strain and serve it. — *Peterson's Magazine.* (*By per. Eds.*)

Eel Soup.

"Put three pounds of small eels in two quarts of water, with a crust of bread, some mace, whole pepper, sweet herbs, and an onion; cover them close, and stew till the fish is quite broken; then strain it off, and serve with some toasted bread cut in slices. It may be thickened with a quarter of a pint of rich cream, and a teaspoonful of flour mixed in it, which is a great improvement."

A Marseilles Receipt for Bouillabaisse.

Almost any sort of fish may be used in making bouillabaisse, and the more kinds the better. Those generally used, because caught in the Mediterranean, are whitings, red mullets, soles, gurnet, turbot, lobsters, and crayfish. Slice two large onions, place them in a wide but deep stewpan made of thin metal; add four or five spoonfuls of the best olive-oil. Fry the onions of a pale brown color. Next place the fish, previously washed and cut in small pieces, in the pan, and cover them with warm water, but not more than equals the depth of the contents; add salt in moderation, half a bay-leaf, and the *flesh* of half a lemon without rind or pips, two tomatoes cut in dice and the seeds removed, a few peppercorns, and four cloves of garlic. Set it on a very hot stove, and let it boil for twelve minutes. By this time the liquor should be reduced to a third of its original quantity; add a small pinch of saffron, a tablespoonful of chopped parsley, and allow it to boil a minute longer; taste, and correct the seasoning if required. Have ready you tureen or deep dish with two dozen slices of light French roll or bread, cut half an inch thick, laid in the bottom; pour some of the soup over, and turn the bread, so that it may be thoroughly soaked; then pour in the remainder, keeping back the inferior parts of the fish, and serve very hot. — DAINTY DISHES: *Lady Harriet St. Clair.*

> A street there is in Paris famous,
>   For which no rhyme our language yields:
> Rue Neuve des Petits Champs its name is —
>   The New Street of the Little Fields;
> And here's an inn, not rich and splendid,
>   But still in comfortable case,
> The which in youth I oft attended,
>   To eat a bowl of Bouillabaisse.
>
> This Bouillabaisse a noble dish is —
>   A sort of soup, or broth, or brew,
> Or hotchpotch of all sorts of fishes,
>   That Greenwich never could outdo;
> Green herbs, red peppers, mussels, saffron,
>   Soles, onions, garlic, roach, and dace;
> All these you eat at Terré's tavern,
>   In that one dish of Bouillabaisse!
>
> *W. M. Thackeray.*

Oyster Soup.

"Take one quart of water, one pint of milk, one small teacup of butter, four crackers rolled fine, one teaspoonful of salt, and half a teaspoonful of pepper. Bring to full boiling-heat as soon as possible, then add one quart of oysters. Let the whole come to a boiling-heat quickly, and remove from the fire."

Mock Oyster Soup.

"One-half pint tomatoes; three-quarters pint of boiling water; butter a quarter size of an egg; a quarter of a teaspoonful each soda, salt, and pepper; one pint sweet milk.

"Put the tomatoes and hot water over the fire, strain, and rub through colander. Meanwhile, boil the milk, stir in soda and butter, and after one boil keep hot (that is, not to let it more than come to the boil). Put pepper and salt with tomatoes, simmer five minutes, and then stir in the milk. Serve with crackers."

Potage à La Reine.

(*Queen Victoria's Favorite Soup.*)

Remove the fat from *one quart* of the water in which *a chicken* has been boiled. Season highly with *salt, pepper,* and *celery-salt,* and a little *onion* if desired, and put on to boil. Mash the yolks of *three hard-boiled eggs* fine, and mix them with *half a cup of bread* or *cracker crumbs* soaked until soft in a little *milk.* Chop the white meat of the chicken until fine like meal, and stir it into the egg and bread paste. Add *one pint* of *hot cream* slowly, and then rub all into the hot chicken liquor. Boil five minutes, add more salt if needed, and if too thick add more cream, or if not thick enough add more fine cracker-dust. It should be like a purée. — THE BOSTON COOK-BOOK : *Mrs. D. A. Lincoln. Roberts Brothers, Pubs.*

Okra or Gumbo Soup.

Boil a chicken and a slice of ham in sufficient water to make a tureen of soup. When the fowl is thoroughly done, take it with the ham from the broth. Flavor the soup with onions, pepper, salt, and sweet herbs; make a paste with eggs and flour, roll it as thin as wafers, dry a little, then roll it as tightly as possible, and slice in thin shreds; put in the soup a teacupful of this, a teacupful of chopped okra, and a pint of oysters. — *Godey's Lady's Book.* (*By per. Pub.*)

Celery Soup.

Three pounds of veal, three bunches of celery, one gallon of water, one teacupful of cream, one tablespoonful of corn-starch; salt and pepper to taste. Put one-half of the celery in the water with the veal, and boil in a closely covered pot for three hours, or until the meat is in pieces. Strain, and return to the pot, and add the remaining half of the celery. Season, and boil twenty minutes longer. Just before taking off of the fire, add the cream, to which has been stirred a tablespoonful of corn-starch. Boil ten minutes longer, and serve with nicely-cut squares of fried toast. — THE KENTUCKY HOUSEKEEPER : *Mrs. Peter A. White.*

Pea Soup.

Use half a pint, or seven ounces, of dried pease (cost three cents), for every two quarts of soup you want. Put them in three quarts of cold water, after washing them well; bring them slowly to a boil; add a bone, or a bit of ham, if you have it to spare, one turnip, and one carrot peeled, one onion stuck with three cloves (cost three cents), and simmer three hours, stirring occasionally to prevent burning; then pass the soup through a sieve with the aid of a potato-masher, and if it shows any sign of settling stir into it one tablespoonful each of butter and flour mixed together dry (cost two cents); this will prevent settling; meantime fry some dice of stale bread, about two slices, cut half an inch square, in hot fat, drain them on a sieve, and put them in the bottom of the soup-tureen in which the pea-soup is served; or cut some bits of very hard stale bread, or dry toast, to use instead of the fried bread. By the time the soup is done, it will have boiled down to two quarts, and will be very thick and good. This receipt will cost you about ten cents. — TWENTY-FIVE-CENT DINNERS: *Miss Juliet Corson.* (*By per. O. Judd Co., Pubs.*)

Corn Soup.

"To each quart of young corn cut from the cob, allow three pints of water. Boil until the grains are tender, and then add two ounces of butter that have been well mixed with one tablespoonful of flour. Let this boil for fifteen minutes longer. Just before serving, add one egg well beaten, and salt and pepper to taste."

A Delicious Soup.

"Peel and slice six large onions, six potatoes, six carrots, and four turnips; fry them in half a pound of butter, and pour on them four quarts of boiling water. Toast a crust of bread as brown and hard as possible, but do not burn it, and put it in, with some celery, sweet herbs, white pepper, and salt. Stew it all gently for four hours, and then strain it through a coarse cloth. Have ready thinly sliced carrot, celery, and a little turnip. Add them to your liking, and stew them tender in the soup. If approved of, a spoonful of tomato catsup may be added."

Croutons,

Or fried bread-crumbs for soups, are prepared in this way: Cut slices of stale home-made bread half an inch thick, trim off all crust, and cut each slice into squares; fry these in very hot fat; drain them on a clean napkin, and add six or eight to each portion of soup. — FIFTY SOUPS: *Thomas J. Murrey. White, Stokes, & Allen, Pubs.*

Marrow Dumplings for Soups.

Grate the crust of a breakfast roll, and break the remainder into crumbs; soak these in cold milk; drain, and add two ounces of flour; chop up half a pound of beef-marrow freed from skin and sinews; beat up the yolks of five eggs; mix all together thoroughly, if too moist add some of the grated crumbs; salt and pepper to taste; form into small round dumplings; boil them in the soup for half an hour before serving. — FIFTY SOUPS: *Thomas J. Murrey. White, Stokes, & Allen, Pubs.*

Vermicelli Soup.

To make vermicelli soup, take as much good stock as you require for your tureen; strain, and set it on the fire, and when it boils put in the vermicelli. Let it simmer for half an hour by a slow fire, that the vermicelli may not break. The soup ought not to be very thick. Half a pound of vermicelli is sufficient for eight or ten persons. — *Godey's Lady's Book.* (*By per. Pub.*)

Noodles for Soup.

Beat up one egg; add a pinch of salt, and flour enough to make a stiff dough; roll out in a very thin sheet; dredge with flour to keep from sticking; then roll up tightly; begin at one end, and shave down fine like cabbage for slaw. — PRESBYTERIAN COOK BOOK, *Dayton, O.* (*By per.*)

CHAPTER II.

FISH AND SHELL-FISH.

FISH AND SHELL-FISH.

We break from the tree-groups, a glade deep with grass;
The white clover's breath loads the sense as we pass.
A sparkle — a streak — a broad glitter is seen,
The bright Callikoon through its thickets of green!
We rush to the banks — its sweet music we hear;
Its gush, dash, and gurgle, all blent to the ear.
No shadows are drawn by the cloud-covered sun.
We plunge in the crystal, our sport is begun.
Our line, where that ripple shoots onward we throw;
It sweeps to the foam-spangled eddy below.
A tremor — a pull — the trout upward is thrown.
He swings to our basket — the prize is our own!
Street.

To Fry Trout.

For those who love the real taste of this excellent fish, there is no better way of dressing them than plain frying. It gives a crispness to the flesh, and leaves its high flavor entire. Cut and clean the trout, wash them, dry them perfectly with napkins; cut the sides and back slightly with a very fine knife, strew a little salt over them, and then dredge them with flour; set on a pan with some clarified butter, and when it is hot lay in the trout; fry them to a delicate brown, and send them up in a napkin, garnished with fried parsley. — VIRGINIA COOKERY-BOOK: *Mrs. Mary Stuart Smith. Harper & Brothers, Pubs. (By per.)*

Green Turtle Steak, Epicurean.

Raw turtle steaks may be had at any first-class restaurant, and occasionally at the fish-stands. It is not advantageous for small families to purchase whole turtles, or rather tortoises, for soup and steaks. Trim away the thigh-bone, and flatten the meat in the form of a steak. Melt two ounces of butter in a chafing-dish; when very hot, add a teaspoonful of Worcestershire sauce, a tablespoonful of currant-jelly, a gill of port wine, and a little salt. Stew the steak in this until tender, and serve from the chafing-dish. — THE BOOK OF ENTRÉES: *Thomas J. Murrey. White, Stokes, & Allen, Pubs.*

Boiled Bass.

Clean and wash the fish, but do not split it or remove the head and tail. Sew up in a piece of mosquito-netting fitted to the shape of the fish. Have in the fish-kettle plenty of boiling water, in which have been mixed a few tablespoonfuls of vinegar, a dozen peppercorns, two or three blades of mace, and a tablespoonful of salt. Cook ten minutes for each pound, and ten minutes over. Undo the cloth, lay the fish on a hot dish, and pour over it a cup of drawn butter seasoned with a tablespoonful of capers and the yolks of two hard-boiled eggs chopped fine. Pass mashed potatoes with it. — *Marion Harland. The Post, Washington, D.C.* (*By per.*)

Roast Sturgeon.

Rub the bottom of the saucepan with a clove of garlic. Put into it a good bit of butter or clarified fat, a pinch of flour, salt and pepper, a chopped onion, and any herb you like the flavor of. Add a half pint of cold water and a gill of vinegar; let it cook all together, stirring it with a wooden spoon. As soon as it is all blended, take it from the fire, and when it is lukewarm put in the thick slices of sturgeon, which you have previously trimmed and cleaned. Let them lie in this sauce for three hours, turning them over now and then. Take from the sauce, drain, and roast on a spit before a slow fire, basting them continually with the sauce. This is the roast fish of the Italian monasteries. It must be served on a very hot dish. — *Public Ledger*, *Philadelphia.* (*By per. Editor of The Household.*)

Salmon Broiled.

Cut the fish in slices from the best part; each slice should be an inch thick; season well with pepper and salt; wrap each slice in white paper which has been buttered with fresh butter; fasten each end by twisting or tying; broil over a very clear fire eight minutes. A coke fire, if kept clear and bright, is best. Serve with butter or tomato-sauce. — AMERICAN HOME COOK-BOOK. *Dick & Fitzgerald, Pubs.* (*By per.*)

Salmon Croquettes.

One pound cooked salmon, or about one and one-half pints when chopped, one cup of cream, two tablespoonfuls butter, one of flour, three eggs, one pint crumbs, pepper, and salt.

This recipe is for cold boiled salmon. A pound can of salmon will not hold the same bulk, as there is always some liquor which must be drained off; so, if canned salmon is used, the cream and other ingredients must be graded in proportion to the bulk of salmon used. Be sure to remove all bits of bone and skin, and then chop the fish.

Add the flour to the butter, and mix thoroughly together. Put the cream into a saucepan, let it come to a boil, and stir in the flour and butter, then the salmon and seasoning. Boil for one minute. Stir into it one well-beaten egg, and remove from the fire. Then set the mixture, which will be quite thin, away on the ice to get perfectly cold. Then shape into croquettes, as with other mixtures, and fry.

Croquettes of any sort are much better if allowed to stand, after being made and shaped, until thoroughly chilled. And when they are put into the frying basket, be careful to let none of them touch each other. — *Mrs. Daniell:* (No. 5) *Boston Cooking School. From The Globe, Boston, Mass.* (*By per.*)

Fillets of Halibut à la Poulette.

Take three pounds of sliced halibut, one-half cupful butter, two large onions, juice of one lemon, three hard-boiled eggs, salt and pepper.

If you buy halibut in a whole piece, pour boiling water over it, and you can then skin it easily. Free the fish from skin and bone, and cut into slices one-half inch thick. Cut these into strips about three inches long and two inches wide. Lay on a platter, and sprinkle with lemon-juice, salt, and pepper, and lay a thin slice of onion on each strip. The lemon-juice had been squeezed out, and was all ready in a cup. If you have to let lemon-juice stand for any length of time, said Mrs. Daniell, be sure you leave no seeds in it, as they will make it bitter. Cover the fish as prepared above, and set away for half an hour.

After the fish has set for half an hour, remove the slices of onion. Have a cup of butter melted in a soup-plate; dip the strips into the butter, roll them up and pin with a little wooden toothpick or skewer; dip in the butter again, and place on a tin pan, and dredge thickly with flour. Bake for twenty minutes in a hot oven. Cut the whites of the eggs into rings, and rub the yolks through a sieve to a fine powder. When the fish is cooked, spread the rolls upon a hot dish, remove the little skewers, pour whip sauce around the fish, scatter the grated yolks over it, and use the whites as a garnish. (Very nice indeed.) — *Mrs. Daniell:* (No. 5) *Boston Cooking School. From Boston Globe.*

Fried Flounders.

Clean the fish, dry them in a cloth, sprinkle with salt, and dredge them well with flour. Put them in hot fat, and fry brown, turning them carefully, so as not to break the fish. — AMERICAN HOME COOK-BOOK.

Broiled Mackerel.

"Prepare, by boiling a short time, a little fennel, parsley, and mint. When done, chop all together fine; mix a piece of butter with it, a dust of flour, pepper, and salt. Cut the fish down the back, and fill it with this stuffing. Oil the gridiron, and oil the fish. Broil over a clear, slow fire."

Fried Whitefish, Fresh.

Hash, and drain well; dredge thickly with flour, and season with salt and pepper. Put on in a skillet containing sufficient *boiling hot* sweet lard; cover, and fry slowly. When a nice brown on one side, turn over, and cook until done. — *Miss Lizzie Strohm.*

Scalloped Fish.

Any cold fresh fish, or cold boiled salt codfish, must be pulled into fine flakes, carefully taking out skin and bones and dark parts; mix in a bowl with equal quantity of bread or cracker crumbs; season with salt, pepper, celery-salt, a little nutmeg, a very little juice squeezed from a cut onion, and a very little red pepper if preferred; moisten the mixture well with a gravy made of melted butter, flour, and hot water; put into a baking-dish, cover with dry crumbs and thickly strewn bits of butter; bake till brown. This is a pretty dish for supper, baked in small tin or earthen shells, or in the great sea-clam shells found on the ocean shore, or in the blue crockery dishes that are sold for such purposes. Serve very hot. — *Mrs. Rose Terry Cooke.* (*By per. Pub. of Good Housekeeping.*)

Fish Jelly.

Take a two-pound haddock, one onion, and half rind lemon; just cover with water, and boil; remove all the bones and skin; flake the fish, or pound it in a mortar, with a tablespoonful of butter, pepper and salt to taste. Put back the bones, reduce the liquor to one pint, add a quarter of a packet of gelatine (previously dissolved in a quarter of a tumbler of cold water). Make some veal forcemeat, without suet, roll in small balls, and drop into boiling water; they will cook in seven minutes. Decorate a mould with the balls and rings of lemon, mix the strained liquor with the pounded fish, and, when nearly cold, pour into the mould. Hard-boiled eggs may be added. Cod or any remains of cold fish can be made over in this way.

To Make a Good Forcemeat.

Chop a slice of lean veal and a slice of boiled ham together, add a bay-leaf crumbled fine, a little sweet basil. — *Public Ledger, Philadelphia.*

Stewed Eels.

"Boil them in a small quantity of water, with some parsley, which should be served up with them and the liquor. Chopped parsley and butter for sauce."

Fried Eels.

Clean and skin the eels. If large, cut them into pieces; if small, skewer them round, and fry them whole. First dust them over with flour, then rub them with the yolk of an egg, and sprinkle them with bread-crumbs. Put them in boiling lard, and fry until nicely browned. — *Peterson's Magazine.* (*By per.*)

Oyster Patties.

Cover small shells or patty-pans with a nice puff paste; bake them well; when done, turn them out on a plate; stew oysters, season them to suit the taste, thicken their juice with egg, and when cold, fill the patties with the oysters.

Oysters Fried to the Queen's Taste.

Small ones are just as toothsome for grilling, but large, plump specimens present a better appearance. Keep if possible a soapstone griddle expressly for cooking them, and let it heat slowly on the back of the range at least an hour before needed. The oysters cannot be drained too long or too well, for one of the secrets of success is to have them perfectly dry. Ten hours is not too long to let them stand in the colander; first place them under a stream of water for three or four minutes to wash off all impurities, wipe lightly afterward with a thin cloth, and place in the ice-chest until wanted; but if desired unexpectedly, sop between towels, lightly patting out the moisture until dry. When ready to cook them, move the griddle to a hot part of the stove, and grease it very slightly with fresh butter; lay on the oysters close together, but not crowding; and as fast as browned nicely, turn them with a spoon, not using a fork, for the piercing lets out the liquor. When done, serve in a very hot dish with a trifle of melted butter. If a griddle cannot be procured, a skillet or frying-pan will answer, and they can either be well shaken all the time, or turned with a spoon. — *Harper's Bazar.* (*By per. Harper & Brothers.*)

Scalloped Oysters.

One pint of oysters (washed), the shells removed, and then drained; one-third of a cup of melted butter, one cup of fine cracker-crumbs moistened in the melted butter; butter a shallow dish, put in a layer of crumbs, then a layer of oysters, season with salt and pepper, and so on, having a thick layer of crumbs on top; bake in a hot oven twenty minutes, or until the cracker is brown. To prepare a larger dish with the same quantity of oysters, heat the oyster-liquor and the butter with an equal quantity of milk, and use more cracker; moisten each layer with the hot liquid; reserve the larger part of the butter for the top layer of crumbs. — *Commercial Gazette, Cincinnati, O. (By per.)*

Broiled Oysters.

Take the largest and finest oysters. See that your gridiron is very clean. Rub the bars with fresh butter, and set it over a clear steady fire, entirely clear from smoke, or on a bed of bright hot wood coals. Place the oysters on the gridiron, and when done on one side, take a fork, and turn them on the other, being careful not to let them burn. Put some fresh butter in the bottom of a dish. Lay the oysters on it, and season them slightly with pepper. Send them to table hot. — AMERICAN HOME COOK-BOOK. (*By per. Dick & Fitzgerald.*)

To Boil Hard-shelled Clams.

"Wash the shells very clean, put them in a pot with as little water as will keep the pot from burning, with their edges down, and boil constantly. When the shells open, they are done; remove them, have ready nice butter toast, and pour the clams on the toast, with as much of the juice as the toast will absorb; add pepper if desired."

Clam Chowder.

"Put in a pot a layer of sliced pork, chopped potatoes, chopped clams, salt, pepper, and lumps of butter, and broken crackers soaked in milk; cover with the clam-juice and water, and stew slowly for three hours; thicken with a little flour; it may be seasoned with spices if preferred."

Clam Scallops.

Chop fifty clams fine, and drain off in a colander all the liquor that will come away. Mix this in a bowl with a cupful of crushed cracker, half a cupful of milk, two beaten eggs, a tablespoonful of melted butter, half a teaspoonful of salt, a pinch of mace and the same of cayenne-pepper. Beat into this the chopped clams, and fill with the mixture clam-shells, or the silver or stone-china shell-shaped dishes sold for this purpose. Bake to a light brown in a quick oven, and serve in the shells. Send around sliced lemon with them. — *Marion Harland. The Post, Washington, D.C.*

Stewed Terrapin.

Of the numerous ways and styles of preparing terrapin, I prefer this one. Select two six-and-a-half to seven inch terrapins; plunge them in boiling water for five minutes; take them out, and when cool, rub off the skin found on the legs and neck;

remove the under-shell carefully; next, remove the liver; cut off the gall-bag from it, and throw it away, for the bursting of the bag would spoil the whole dish. The other parts to be rejected are the claws, head, and sand-bag; the remainder should be cut into neat-sized pieces. Put these in a stewpan or chafing-dish, and stew long enough to become tender — about one-half to three quarters of an hour. Now put in a chafing-dish a pat of butter rolled in a little flour, a dash of cayenne, a gill of sherry, two drops of soy, and a saltspoonful of salt. When hot beat it with a fork, and add the terrapin, and eggs if there are any. The creamy sauce so universally met with consists of a combination of cream, butter, and eggs, which is very nice for those who like that sort of thing. — THE BOOK OF ENTRÉES: *Thomas J. Murrey. White, Stokes, & Allen, Pubs.*

Lobster Chowder.

Meat of one fine lobster, picked out from the shell and cut into bits, one quart of milk, six Boston crackers split and buttered, one even teaspoonful of salt, one scant quarter-teaspoonful of cayenne, two tablespoonfuls of butter rolled in one of prepared flour, a pinch of soda in the milk. Scald the milk, and stir in seasoning, butter, and flour, cook one minute, add the lobster, and simmer five minutes. Line a tureen with the toasted and buttered crackers, dipping each quickly in boiling water before putting it in place, and pour in the chowder. Send around sliced lemon with it. — *Marion Harland. The Post, Washington, D.C.* (*By per.*)

Lobster Sauce.

One small lobster, four tablespoonfuls of butter, two of flour, one-fifth of a teaspoonful of cayenne, two tablespoonfuls of lemon-juice, one pint of boiling water. Cut the meat into dice. Pound the "coral" with one tablespoonful of the butter. Rub the flour and the remainder of the butter to a smooth paste. Add the water, pounded "coral," and butter, and the seasoning. Simmer five minutes, and then strain on the lobster. Boil up once, and serve. This sauce is for all kinds of boiled fish. — NEW COOK-BOOK : *Miss Maria Parloa. Estes & Lauriat, Pubs.* (*By per.*)

CHAPTER III.

BEEF, VEAL, LAMB, AND MUTTON.

BEEF, VEAL, LAMB, AND MUTTON.

"Tell me, dearest husband," Kitty said,
  "Before you go, I pray,
How shall I get the meat and bread
  For our noon meal to-day?"

"Buy them with smiles," the husband cried;
  "But that won't pay," says she.
"Then take this kiss," her lord replied,
  And to his shop went he.

The noontime came, and he came too;
  And the dinner was prepared.
A tender steak was in full view,
  "Quite splendid," he declared.

He said he wished to have such meat
  Three times a day in future;
"But tell me, love, for this great treat
  What did you pay the butcher?"

"What did I pay? I paid the kiss —
  'Twas all you left, you know."
"A-a-ll right," said he; "but, after this,
  Take money when you go."
            Kisses at Market: *Anon.*

French Beefsteak.

"Cut the steak two-thirds of an inch thick from a fillet of beef; dip into melted fresh butter, lay them on a heated gridiron, and broil over hot coals. When nearly done, sprinkle pepper and salt. Have ready some parsley chopped fine, and mixed with softened butter. Beat them together to a cream, and pour into the middle of the dish. Dip each steak into the butter, turning them over, and lay them round on the platter. If liked, squeeze a few drops of lemon over, and serve very hot."

A Spanish Steak.

"Take the tenderloin of beef. Have onions cut fine, and put into a frying-pan with some boiling butter. When quite soft, draw them to the back part of the pan, and, having seasoned well the beef with pepper and salt, put it in the pan, and rather broil than fry it. When done, put the onions over it, and just as much boiling water as will make a gravy. Let it stew a few minutes."

Roast Beef.

Prepare for the oven by dredging lightly with flour, and seasoning with salt and pepper; place in the oven, and baste frequently while roasting. Allow a quarter of an hour for a pound of meat, if you like it rare; longer, if you like it well done. Serve with a sauce made from the drippings in the pan, to which have been added a tablespoonful of Harvey or Worcestershire sauce and a tablespoonful of tomato catsup. — EVERY-DAY COOK-BOOK: *Miss Neill.* (*By per. Belford, Clarke, & Co.*)

Fried Beefsteaks.

Place the steak in a pan in which is an ounce of hot butter or fat. Fry ten or twelve minutes, turning on each side three times, and watching that the meat does not burn. Season with salt and pepper. After removing the meat, a gravy may be made by adding a little water, and thickening with flour rubbed smooth in water. — *Arthur's Home Magazine.* (*By per.*)

Beef à la Mode.

Take three pounds of fresh beef, trim off the fat; cut half a pound of bacon into long, slender strips, and lard the beef with it. Mix a few cloves, mace, allspice, peppers, cayenne, tablespoonful of powdered thyme, and two cloves of garlic, with half a pint of malt vinegar. Put the meat into an earthen crock, with a thin slice of bacon under it, add the seasoning and a pint of soup-stock, cover the crock, and simmer six hours. When preferred, vegetables may be added, but it is more satisfactory to cook them separately. — THE BOOK OF ENTRÉES: *Thomas J. Murrey. White, Stokes, & Allen, Pubs.*

Beef Stew or Hash.

"Take a pound of cold boiled beef, and slice into small bits. Put on to stew with six or eight medium-sized potatoes and three large onions peeled and cut into small pieces. Have sufficient water, that, when done, it will be rather juicy than dry. Season with salt and pepper, and add a little butter, if the meat does not make it rich enough." This is a plain but savory stew.

Beefsteak Pie.

A good common paste for meat pies, and which is intended to be eaten, is made as follows: Three ounces of butter and one pound of flour will be sufficient for one dish. Rub the butter well amongst the flour so as to incorporate them thoroughly. If the butter be fresh, add a little salt. Mix up the flour and butter with as much cold water as will make a thick paste. Knead it quickly on a board, and roll it out flat with a rolling-pin. Turn the dish upside down upon the flattened paste, and cut or shape out the piece required for the cover. Roll out the parings, and cut them into strips. Wet the edges of the dish, and place these strips neatly round on the edges as a foundation for the cover. Then take some slices of tender beef mixed with fat; those from the rump are the best. Season them with pepper and salt, and roll each slice up in a small bundle, or lay them flat in the dish. Put in a little gravy or cold water, and a little flour for thickening. Then, after putting in the meat, lay the cover on the dish, pressing down the edges closely to keep all tight. If any paste remain, cut or stamp it into ornaments, such as leaves, and place these as a decoration on the cover.

On taking pies from the oven, and while quite hot, the crust may be glazed with white of egg and water beaten together, or sugar and water laid on with a brush. — AMERICAN HOME COOK-BOOK. (*By per. Dick & Fitzgerald, Pubs.*)

Such a busy little woman as she was! So full of self-importance, and trying so hard not to smile or seem uncertain about any thing. It was a perfect treat to Tom to see her with her brows knit, and her rosy lips pursed up, kneading away at the crust, rolling it out, cutting it up into strips, lining the basin with it, shaving it off fine round the rim; chopping up the steak into small pieces, raining down pepper and salt upon them, packing them into the basin, pouring in cold water for gravy; and never venturing to steal a look in his direction, lest her gravity should be disturbed; until at last, the basin being quite full and only wanting the top crust, she clapped her hands, all covered with paste and flour, at Tom, and burst out heartily into such a charming little laugh of triumph, that the pudding need have had no other seasoning to commend it to the taste of any reasonable man on earth. — MARTIN CHUZZLEWIT: *Charles Dickens.*

Yorkshire Pudding with Roast Beef.

"Five tablespoonfuls of flour mixed with one of salt, one pint of milk, and three well-beaten eggs. Butter a square pan, and put the batter in it; set it in the oven until it rises and is slightly crusted on the top; then place it under your beef roasting before the fire, or in the oven, and baste it as you do your meat. In serving, cut it in squares, and lay around the meat in the dish."

Beef Loaf.

Chop very fine, or have your butcher mince, two pounds of coarse, lean beef. Season spicily with pepper, salt, nutmeg, summer savory or sweet marjoram, and a cautious sprinkling of minced onion. Beat two eggs light, and work up with the mass. Press hard into a bowl; fit a saucer or plate (inverted) upon the meat, and set in a dripping-pan of boiling water to cook slowly for an hour and a quarter. Lay a weight on the surface when it is done, and let it get perfectly cold before turning out. Cut in perpendicular slices. — *Marion Harland. The Post, Washington, D.C. (By per.)*

Frizzled Dried Beef.

Cut your beef very thin, then pull it into small pieces, taking out all the strings of sinew, fat, and bits of outside; put it in a frying-pan, and cover with cold water; let it simmer on the back of the stove till perfectly tender; then pour off the water, and cover the beef with cream, add pepper, celery-salt, and salt if needed; mix one tablespoonful of melted butter with one heaped tablespoon of flour, and stir into the hot cream; cover, and keep very hot till served. — *Mrs. Rose Terry Cooke.* (*By per. Pub. of Good Housekeeping.*)

To Boil Tongue.

"A tongue is so hard, whether prepared by drying or pickling, that it requires much more cooking than a ham: nothing of its weight takes so long to dress properly.

"A tongue that has been salted and dried should be put to soak (if it is old and very hard, twenty-four hours before it is wanted) in plenty of water; one fresh from the pickle requires soaking only a few hours. Put the tongue into plenty of cold water, with a bunch of savory herbs, let it be an hour gradually warming, and give it from three and a half to four hours very slow simmering, according to the size.

"When you choose a tongue, endeavor to learn how long it has been dried or pickled; pick out the plumpest and that which has the smoothest skin, which denotes its being young and tender."

Ragout of Liver.

Heat three or four spoonfuls of nice dripping in a frying-pan; add an onion sliced, a tablespoonful of chopped parsley, and thrice as much minced breakfast-bacon; when all are hissing hot, lay in the liver cut in pieces as long and wide as your middle finger, and fry brown, turning often; take out the liver, and keep warm in a covered hot-water dish; strain the gravy, rinse out the frying-pan, and return to the fire with the gravy and an even tablespoonful of butter worked up well in two of browned flour. Stir until you have a smooth browned roux; thin gradually with half a cupful of boiling water and the juice of half a lemon, add a teaspoonful of minced pickle and a scant half-teaspoonful of curry-powder wet with cold water. Boil sharply, pour over the liver; put fresh boiling water in the pan under the dish, and let all stand closely covered for ten minutes before serving. — *Marion Harland. The Post, Washington, D.C.*

Veal Sweetbread.

"Trim a fine sweetbread; parboil it for five minutes, and throw it into a basin of cold water. When the sweetbread is cold, dry it thoroughly in a cloth; run a skewer through it; egg it with a paste-brush, powder it well with bread-crumbs, and roast it."

Fricandeau à l'Oseille.

Procure a piece of veal cut from the leg, and about one inch and a half in thickness; the small round bone in the middle may be either left or removed. Lard it well with salt pork; put into a bake-pan one ounce of salt pork to two pounds of veal, two or three slices of onion, as many of carrot, as many sprigs of parsley, and half a bay-leaf; lay the veal over the whole; add just broth enough to cover the bottom of the pan, and a little salt; set in the oven, and baste now and then. If the juice is absorbed, and there is not enough to baste, add a little more broth.

Bear in mind that veal must always be overdone. Serve on a *purée* of sorrel. — *Pierre Blot.*

Purée d'Oseille (Purée of Sorrel).

Throw the sorrel, when cleaned and washed, into boiling water; at the first boiling, and as soon as tender, turn into a colander; press it to extract the water, and then chop it. Put it in a saucepan on the fire, with a piece of butter, and stir for five minutes; add a little broth; stir another five minutes, spread it around a dish, place the veal in the middle, pour the gravy all over it, and serve. — *Pierre Blot.*

Stewed Veal.

"Cut the veal in small bits, stew in a little water with butter, pepper, and salt, until tender; thicken with a little flour."

Braised Veal.

Chop a half pound of fat salt pork fine, and put half of it in the bottom of a broad pot; sprinkle it with minced onion, sweet herbs, and a teaspoonful of chopped carrot. Lay a breast of veal on this bed, and cover it with a similar layer. Pour in carefully a quart of weak broth, if you have it; if not, cold water; season with pepper and salt. Fit a tight lid on the pot, and set where it will cook slowly — very slowly — for two hours at least. Now take up the meat, rub butter all over it, and dredge thickly with browned flour. Put it into a dripping-pan; strain the gravy from the pot into tins, not pouring it on the meat, and bake half an hour in a good oven, basting every five minutes with the gravy. Transfer the veal to a hot dish; thicken the gravy in the pan with browned flour wet with cold water, boil up, and serve in a boat. — *Marion Harland.* *The Post, Washington, D.C.*

Veal and Rice.

Put the scrag end of a neck of veal, which you can usually buy for ten cents, into a pot half full of boiling water, with a half tablespoonful of salt, and half a pound of bacon or salt pork (cost six cents), half a pound of rice (cost five cents), and an onion stuck with six cloves; boil it gently for three hours, and then serve it hot; put the meat in the middle of the platter, and the rice laid around it. — TWENTY-FIVE-CENT DINNERS: *Miss Juliet Corson.* (*By per.*)

Mutton au Chou.

Bake a leg or a breast of mutton in the oven, basting it well, and half an hour before it is done put in the pan a cabbage, chopped fine as for cold slaw. The cabbage will cook in the rich gravy, and the basting must be continued so as to give the gravy all possible taste of the osmazome of the meat, — the browned crust that gives the flavor and pleasant odor in all roasting or baking meats.—*Philadelphia Ledger.* (*By per.*)

Mutton Steaks.

"They should be broiled over a clear fire, seasoned when half done, and often turned. Take them up into a very hot dish, rub a little butter over them, and serve quite hot."

Stewed Shoulder of Mutton.

"Select a shoulder of mutton that is not too fat; bone it, tie in a cloth, and boil it for two hours and a half. Take it up, put a little cold butter over it, and then strew thickly with bread-crumbs and parsley, with pepper and salt, all properly mixed; and let it remain in the oven half an hour to be perfectly browned."

A man may feel thankful, heartily thankful, over a dish of plain mutton with turnips. — GRACE BEFORE MEAT: *Charles Lamb.*

Irish Stew.

Cut a neck of mutton in pieces, blanch the chops in water, take and put them into another stewpan with four onions cut in slices; put to it a little stock; let it boil a quarter of an hour; have ready some potatoes pared; put them into the stewpan with the mutton, with salt and pepper. As some like the potatoes whole, and some mashed, to thicken the stew, you must boil them accordingly. Dish the meat round, and the vegetables in the middle. — *Arthur's Home Magazine.*

Breast of Lamb, with Peas.

This part of the lamb is always cheaper than other portions, and not only has this to recommend it, but is readily adaptable to many delicate and palate-pleasing dishes, one of which is the following: Trim off the skin and part of the fat from the breast of a spring lamb; cut the meat into squares or triangular pieces; dredge in flour; put them into a stewpan with a small quantity of butter and herb seasonings; toss them about, and brown them nicely; add a pint of soup-stock to each pound of meat; simmer until tender, and skim off all surplus fat. Just before serving, add half a can of French peas, pour out on a hot dish, garnish with large *croutons*, and serve. The tops of asparagus, French beans, etc., may be used instead of peas. — THE BOOK OF ENTRÉES : *Thomas J. Murrey. White, Stokes, & Allen, Pubs.*

Lamb Chops.

Fry them a light brown, in butter, then add a little water, flour, salt, and a dust of pepper, to the gravy; let it brown, and pour it over the chops. —*From Peterson's Magazine.* (*By per.*)

To Roast Lamb.

The hind-quarter of lamb usually weighs from seven to ten pounds; this size will take about two hours to roast it. Have a brisk fire. It must be very frequently basted while roasting, and sprinkled with a little salt, and dredged all over with flour, about half an hour before it is done.

All joints of roast lamb may be garnished with double parsley, and served up with either asparagus and new potatoes, spring spinach and new potatoes, green peas and new potatoes, or with cauliflowers or French beans and potatoes; and never forget to send up mint sauce. The following will be found an excellent receipt for mint sauce : With three heaped tablespoonfuls of finely chopped young mint, mix two of pounded and sifted sugar, and six of the best vinegar; stir it until the sugar is dissolved. — *Godey's Lady's Book.* (*By per.*)

CHAPTER IV.

PORK.

PORK.

Of all the delicacies in the whole *mundus edibilis*, I will maintain it to be the most delicate — *princeps obsoniorum*. . . . There is no flavor comparable, I will contend, to that of the crisp, tawny, well-watched, not over-roasted, *crackling*, as it is well called, — the very teeth are invited to their share of the pleasure at this banquet in overcoming the coy, brittle resistance, — with the adhesive oleaginous — oh, call it not fat, but an indefinable sweetness growing up to it; the tender blossoming of fat; fat cropped in the bud, taken in the shoot, in the first innocence; the cream and quintessence of the child-pig's yet pure food; the lean, no lean, but a kind of animal manna; or rather, fat and lean (if it must be so) so blended and running into each other, that both together make but one ambrosial result, or common substance. — A Dissertation upon Roast Pig: *Charles Lamb.*

Roast Pig.

Soak in milk some light bread; boil some sage and onions in plenty of water, strain it off, and chop it very fine; press the milk from the bread, and then mix the sage and onion with pepper and salt; in the bread put the yolk of an egg to bind it a little; put this in the inside of the pig; rub the pig over with milk and butter, paper it, roast it a beautiful brown. Cut off the head before it is drawn from the spit, and likewise cut it down the back, and then you will not break the skin: take out the spit, cut off the ears from the head, and crack the bone, and take out the brains; put them in a stewpan with all the inside stuffing and a little brown sauce; dish the pig, the back outside, and put the sauce in the middle and some in a boat, the ears at each end. — American Home Cook-Book. *Dick & Fitzgerald, Pubs. (By per.)*

Spare-Rib.

A spare-rib will take two hours and a half to roast; if very large, three hours. If not already salted, sprinkle with some, and while roasting baste with butter and dredge with flour; about twenty minutes before it is done, sift a little powdered sage over it. — *Arthur's Home Magazine.*

Pork Steaks.

"Cut them from a loin or neck, not too thick, pepper and broil them, turning often; when nearly done, add salt, rub a piece of butter over, and serve hot."

Tenderloin on Toast.

"Cut pork tenderloins in very thin slices; stew them in a little water till they are nearly done; then put a little butter in a saucepan, and fry them till light brown. Serve on buttered toast and raw tomatoes sliced thin."

Pork Fritters.

Have at hand a thick batter of Indian meal and flour; cut a few slices of pork, and fry them in the frying-pan until the fat is fried out; cut a few more slices of the pork, dip them in the batter, and drop them in the bubbling fat, seasoning with salt and pepper; cook until brown, and eat while hot. — EVERY-DAY COOK-BOOK: *Miss E. Neill.*

Salt Pork and Apples.

"Cut half a pound of nicely cured pork in slices a quarter of an inch thick, fry them slowly until brown in a deep frying-pan, and take them up on a hot dish.

Meantime wash, wipe, and slice six sour apples, and when the pork is taken up put them into the frying-pan to cook until they are tender, but not broken. Lay them on a dish with the pork, and serve them hot."

Bacon and Eggs.

Take a quarter of a pound of streaked bacon, cut it into thin slices, and put them into a frying-pan over a slow fire; take care to turn them frequently; when the meat is done, take it out, and break into the hot fat seven or eight eggs. Cook more or less according to taste, and serve with the bacon. — *Arthur's Home Magazine.*

>Oh! 'tis eggs are a treat,
>When so white and so sweet,
>From under the manger they're taken,
>And by fair Margery —
>Och! 'tis she's full of glee —
>They are fried with fat rashers of bacon.
>*Father Prout's Relics.*

To Boil Pickled Pork.

Having washed and scraped it, put it into boiling water with the skin-side uppermost. If it be thin, a piece of four pounds will be done in less than an hour; a leg of eight pounds will take three hours. Pork should be done enough, but if boiled too fast or too long it will become jelly. Keep the pot well skimmed, and send it to table with peas-pudding and greens. Some persons like carrots, parsnips also. — AMERICAN HOME COOK-BOOK. *Dick & Fitzgerald, Pubs. (By per.)*

Soused Pig's Feet.

Take the ears, feet, and upper part of the head; scrape clean, boil until the meat is tender; take it up; flavor properly, and put into pure vinegar; spice as you like. Put it in a jar, and keep closely covered. Tripe can be pickled in the same way. — AMERICAN HOME COOK-BOOK.

Jelly of Pig's Feet and Ears.

Clean and prepare as for soused pig's feet, then boil them in a very small quantity of water till every bone can be taken out; throw in half a handful of chopped sage, the same of parsley, and a seasoning of pepper, salt, and mace, in fine powder; simmer till the herbs are scalded, then pour the whole into a melon form. — AMERICAN HOME COOK-BOOK.

To Boil a Ham.

If the ham has been long cured, soak it in cold water for from twelve to twenty hours. Scrape it, and put it into a large vessel to boil with plenty of cold water, and let it simmer gently from three to four or five hours according to the size. A ham of twenty pounds will require four hours and a half. Skim the pot frequently to remove the grease as it rises. When done, strip off the rind, and strew bread-raspings over the top side, then set it before the fire, or in the oven, to dry and brown. — AMERICAN HOME COOK-BOOK.

To Broil Ham.

Cut the ham about a third of an inch thick, and broil it very quickly over a brisk fire; lay it on a hot dish, pepper it, and put on it a good lump of butter. — AMERICAN HOME COOK-BOOK.

CHAPTER V.

MISCELLANEOUS.

MISCELLANEOUS.

Two swift-winged hours will bring the time
When sounds the sabbath supper chime;
And I'll desert my easy nest
To reach the board before the rest, —
To reach the board so white and neat,
That I may something have to eat.

I know just what the feast will be:
Some bread cut thin, and weakly tea,
Some cheap and highly-colored jam,
Some slices of transparent ham,
Some Gorgonzola, — Jersey make, —
Some tiny bits of frosted cake.

The napery will be as white
As all the silverware is bright;
The cups and saucers, fragile, thin,
Would suit a captious mandarin;
And then the waiter, black as night,
Will be both constant and polite.

To cheer the fond æsthetic heart,
The boarders will converse on art,
The drama, music, poesy,
And politics, to-night at tea;
And Clara Vere de Vere will chat
About the latest Paris hat.

A good meal makes a merrier heart
Than all your high æsthetic art.
When one is hungry, frescoed walls
Can't take the place of codfish balls;
No substitutes are painted screens
And porcelain, for pork and beans;
A banquet may be all that's sweet,
Even though all be incomplete
That's alien to the things to eat.

THE SABBATH SUPPER CHIME: *Puck*. (*By per. Ed.*)

Codfish Balls.

Pick up as fine as possible a teacup of nice white codfish. Freshen all night, or, if wanted for any other meal than breakfast, from the morning; scald it once, and drain off the water; chop and work it until entirely fine; put it in a basin with water, a bit of butter the size of an egg, and two eggs; beat it thoroughly, and heat it until it thickens, without boiling. It should, when all is mixed, be about a quart. Have some potatoes ready prepared and nicely mashed; work the fish and potatoes thoroughly together as above, make it in flat cakes, and brown both sides. This is a very nice dish, as all who have tried it allow. — *Godey's Lady's Book.* (*By per. Pub.*)

Baked Beans.

The small white beans are the best for baking. Pick out the bad ones; wash, and soak over night in lukewarm water. Early the next morning set them where they will boil, adding a teaspoonful of saleratus. When partially done, take them out of the water with a skimmer, and put them in an earthen jar or crock, salting them at the same time. Gash about a pound of pork in narrow strips, put it with the beans in such a way that all the rind will be covered. Turn in water until you can just see it at the top. Bake the beans from two to five hours in a moderate oven. The beans when done should be of a nice even brown over the top, the pork tender, and the rind crispy. — *Arthur's Home Magazine.* (*By per. Pubs.*)

"Liver?" said Toby, communing with himself. "No, there's a mildness about it that don't answer to liver. Pettitoes? No. It ain't faint enough for pettitoes. It wants the stringiness of cocks' heads. And I know it ain't sausages. I'll tell you what it is. It's chitterlings!"

"No, it ain't!" cried Meg, in a burst of delight. "No, it ain't!"

"Why, what am I a-thinking of!" said Toby, suddenly recovering a position as near the perpendicular as it was possible for him to assume. "I shall forget my own name next. It's tripe."

Tripe it was; and Meg, in high joy, protested he should say, in half a minute more, it was the best tripe ever stewed. — THE CHIMES: *Charles Dickens.*

Stewed Tripe.

Select two pounds of double tripe well cleaned and blanched, cut in pieces of rather less than a quarter of a pound each; put in a clean stewpan with a pint of milk and one of water, two teaspoonfuls of salt, one of pepper, eight middle-sized onions carefully peeled. Set it on to boil, which it should do at first rather fast, then simmer till done, which will be in rather more than half an hour. Put it into a deep dish or tureen, and serve with the milk and onions. — DAINTY DISHES: *Lady Harriet St. Clair.*

Pettitoes.

"Boil them, the liver, and the heart, very gently in a little water; then mince the meat fine, split the feet, and simmer till they are tender; thicken with flour, butter, and a spoonful of cream; add salt and pepper, let it boil, pour it over a few sippets of bread, and put the feet on the mince."

Sausages.

"The proper seasoning is salt, pepper, sage, summer savory, or thyme; they should be one-third fat, the remainder lean, finely chopped, and the seasonings well mixed, and proportioned so that one herb may not predominate over the others. If skins are used, they cannot be prepared with too much care; but they are about as well made into cakes."

To keep Sausage Fresh all the Year.

"Fry as if for present use; pack in stone jars, and, if the grease that fries out of the meat is not sufficient to cover it, pour over hot lard so as to cover it, and entirely exclude the air."

White or Suet Pudding.

Two pounds of suet, four pounds of flour. Rub the suet thoroughly in the flour, until *well mixed.* Season with salt and pepper; spice with a heaping tablespoonful of cinnamon. Make little muslin bags that will hold about a teacupful of the mixture. Fill them, tie tightly, and boil slowly about half an hour. Drain them off, and when dry spread out on shallow dishes, and keep in a good cupboard. When desired to use, take one or more, as may be required, re-boil a while, then remove the muslin, and put the pudding on a patty-pan or baking-dish, and set in the oven a short time to brown. Send to the table hot. It is very nice to use for breakfast sometimes, taking the place of sausages, hash, and kindred dishes.

To bake a Beef's Heart.

Cut it open, remove the ventricles, and let it soak an hour in lukewarm water. Wipe dry with a cloth, and parboil for twenty minutes. Make a rich stuffing, fill the heart with it, and secure it with a string. Let it bake an hour and a half or two hours, with half a pint of water in the pan. The gravy will not need any thickening. Serve with currant or any acid jelly. — *Arthur's Home Magazine.* (*By per.*)

Lamb's Head.

"Soak the head well in cold water, and boil it separately till very tender. Parboil the liver and lights, mince them small, and stir them in a little of the water in which they were boiled; add seasoning, thicken with floured butter, and serve the head with the mince around it."

Little Pigs in Blankets.

Season large oysters with salt and pepper. Cut fat English bacon in very thin slices; wrap an oyster in each slice, and fasten with a little wooden skewer (tooth-picks are the best things). Heat a frying-pan, and put in the "little pigs." Cook just long enough to crisp the bacon, — about two minutes. Place on slices of toast that have been cut into small pieces, and serve immediately. Do not remove the skewers. This is a nice relish for lunch or tea; and, garnished with parsley, is a pretty one. The pan must be very hot before the "pigs" are put in, and then great care must be taken that they do not burn. — NEW COOK-BOOK: *Miss Maria Parloa. Estes & Lauriat, Pubs.* (*By per.*)

"Bubble and Squeak."

Take from a round of beef, which has been well boiled and cold, two or three slices, amounting to about one pound to one pound and a half in weight, two carrots which have been boiled with the joint, in a cold state, as also the hearts of two boiled greens that are cold. Cut the meat into small dice-formed pieces, and chop up the vegetables together; pepper and salt the latter, and fry them with the meat in a pan in a quarter-pound of sweet butter; when fully done, add to the pan in which the ingredients are fried, half a gill of fresh catsup, and serve your dish up to the dinner-table with mashed potatoes. — *Godey's Lady's Book.* (*By per.*)

Meat Porcupine.

Chop fine some *lean cooked veal, chicken,* or *lamb;* and *one-fourth* its amount of *cracker* or *bread crumbs* or *mashed potato,* and a small quantity of *chopped bacon;* season highly with *salt, pepper, cayenne,* and *lemon-juice;* moisten with *beaten egg* and *stock* or *water* enough to shape it. Mould it into an oval loaf, and put into a shallow pan well greased. Cut strips of *fat bacon* one-fourth of an inch wide and one inch long. Make holes in the loaf with a small skewer; insert the strips of bacon, leaving the ends out half an inch, and push the meat up firmly round the bacon. Bake till brown. The bacon will baste the meat sufficiently. — THE BOSTON COOK-BOOK: *Mrs. D. A. Lincoln. Roberts Brothers, Pubs.* (*By per.*)

Hints for Marketing.

"Good fresh beef has a fine grain, and is of a rich carnation color. It is firm, but tender and elastic to the touch. The fat is yellowish white and firm.

"Veal should have firm white fat, and the lean have a pinkish tinge.

"The best mutton is of a fine grain, a bright color, the fat firm and white.

"Lamb should be eaten very fresh. In the forequarter, the vein in the neck being any other color than blue betrays it to be stale.

"Pork, when fresh and young, is smooth and firm, and the rind is thin. The lean must be of a uniform color, and the fat white and not at all streaked.

"A good test for ham is to run a knife under the bone; if it comes out clean, and smells agreeably, the ham is good.

"In the selection of fish, make sure that the eyes are full, the gills bright red, and the flesh firm and stiff. If the flesh is flabby, the eyes sunken, and the gills of a dark color, the fish is stale. They should be thoroughly cleaned when first procured, and washed in just sufficient water to cleanse them. If much water is used, the flavor will be diminished. Sprinkle salt in the inside, and if they are to be broiled, add pepper. Keep them in a cool place till you wish to cook them. Fresh-water fish are apt to have an earthy taste, which may be removed by soaking them in salt and water after cleaning. Most kinds of salt fish should be soaked in cold water ten or twelve hours before cooking.

"Flat fish, as a rule, keep better than round. They should be chosen for their thickness rather than for their size."

CHAPTER VI.

POULTRY.

POULTRY.

SAM LAWSON AND HIS TURKEY.

"THERE, to be sure," said Aunt Lois, one day when our preparations were in full blast, "there comes Sam Lawson down the hill, limpsy as ever; now he'll have his doleful story to tell, and mother'll give him one of the turkeys."

And so, of course, it fell out. Sam came in with his usual air of plaintive assurance, and seated himself a contemplative spectator in the chimney-corner, regardless of the looks and signs of unwelcome on the part of Aunt Lois.

"Lordy massy, how prosperous every thing does seem here!" he said in musing tones, over his inevitable mug of cider; "so different from what 'tis t' our home. There's Hepsy, she's all in a stew, an' I've just been an' got her thirty-seven cents wuth o' nutmegs, yet she says she's sure she don't see how she's to keep Thanksgiving, an' she's down on me about it, just as ef 'twas my fault. Yeh see, last winter, our old gobbler got froze. You know, Mis' Badger, that 'ere cold night we had last winter. Wal, I was off with Jake Marshall that night: ye see, Jake, he hed to take old Gen. Dearborn's corpse into Boston, to the family vault, an' Jake, he kind o' hated to go alone. 'Twas a dreful cold time, an' he ses to me, 'Sam, you jes' go 'long with me.' So I was sort o' sorry for him, an' I kind o' thought I'd go 'long. Wal, come 'long to Josh Bissel's tahvern, there at the Half-way House, you know, 'twas so swinging cold, we stopped to take a little suthin' warmin', an' we sort o' sot an' sot over the fire, till, first we knew, we kind o' got asleep; an' when we woke up, we found we'd left the old general hitched up t' th' post pretty much all night. Wal, didn't hurt him none, poor man; 'twas allers a favorite spot o' his'n. But, takin' one thing with another, I didn't get home till about noon next day, an' I tell you, Hepsy, she was right down on me. She said the baby was sick, an' there hadn't been no wood split, nor the barn fastened up, nor nothin'! Lordy massy, I didn't mean no harm. I thought there was wood enough, an' I thought likely Hepsy'd git out an' fasten up the barn. But Hepsy, she was in one o' her contrary streaks, an' she wouldn't do a thing. An' when I went out to look, why, sure 'nuff, there was our old tom-turkey froze as stiff as a stake, — his claws jist a-stickin' right straight up like this." Here Sam struck an expressive attitude, and looked so much like a frozen turkey, as to give a pathetic reality to the picture.

"Well, now, Sam, why need you be off on things that's none of your business?" said my grandmother. "I've talked to you plainly about that a great many times, Sam," she continued, in tones of severe admonition. "Hepsy is a hard-working woman, but she can't be expected to see to every thing; an' you oughter 'ave been at home that night to fasten up your own barn, and look after your own creeturs."

Sam took the rebuke all the more meekly, as he perceived the stiff black legs of a turkey poking out from under my grandmother's apron, while she was delivering it. To be exhorted and told of his shortcomings, and then furnished with a turkey at Thanksgiving, was a yearly part of his family programme. In time he departed, not only with the turkey, but with us boys in procession after him, bearing a mince and a pumpkin pie for Hepsy's children.

"Poor things!" my grandmother remarked; "they ought to have something good to eat Thanksgiving Day; 'tain't their fault that they've got a shiftless father." — OLDTOWN FOLKS: *Mrs. H. B. Stowe. Houghton, Mifflin, & Co., Pubs.* (*By per.*)

How to Select a Turkey.

The practice of sending partially dressed fowls to our markets is one which should be condemned by every housekeeper who desires pure, untainted meat. Therefore, in the selection of a turkey, first see that it is entirely cleansed inside; and especially see that the crop is removed, as this, with its undigested food, will very soon poison the whole of the most delicious portion of the fowl. The skin should be of fine texture, and should disclose no purple flesh underneath, as that indicates age. The legs should be smooth and dark, and the spurs soft and loose. There should be no heavy layers of pale, unhealthy fat along the back: this indicates a rapidly fattened, if not a stall-fed turkey. The flesh must be white and the breast plump, and the fat yellow; but, above all, it should smell perfectly sweet inside. Having secured a good turkey, the next thing to do is to thoroughly cleanse it, extract the pin-feathers, and hang it up to dry.

How to Roast a Turkey.

While it is drying, prepare a dressing in the following manner: If you have no good home-made loaf, take one-half or three-fourths of a stale loaf of baker's bread, and cut into small pieces, over which pour very scantily warm (not boiling) water; enough to make the bread light, soft, and still have it flaky, is the desired quantity; boiling water poured over bread until it is mushy and glutinous will never make good stuffing; add two well-beaten eggs, a good pinch of finely powdered sage without the stems, one small onion fried a golden brown in butter, pepper and salt. Now put into a skillet a tablespoonful of butter, and, when turning a light brown, add the dressing; leave it to fry a golden brown, then turn and stir until thoroughly heated. Take it off, and fill the turkey, after salting the inside; do not press the dressing in compactly, but leave room for it to swell. It should have been said at the proper place, to push back the skin from the neck, and cut the latter off close to the body; stuff the breast from this opening, then turn the skin over on the back, and sew it; the other vent needs no sewing, when the fowl is properly stuffed; now press the legs up as far as possible toward the breast, and secure firmly to the end of the turkey. With a rubbing over of salt, it is now ready for the oven, and if roasted in an enclosed pan, there will be no need of basting; otherwise, with about a half-pint of water to start it, it will need to be basted frequently. The heat of the oven should be moderate at first, but increased afterward; if it browns too fast, wet a clean cloth in water, and lay over the turkey; this can be remoistened occasionally. Allow about twenty minutes to each pound of meat. When the turkey is taken out, there should be nothing but fat in the pan with which to make gravy; if there is more than three or four tablespoonfuls, pour it out, as that is sufficient; into what is left in the pan, put flour enough to absorb it, and let it cook, with constant stirring, until the flour is done; then add a pint and a half of *cold* water, and stir constantly until it thickens. To insure good gravy, the fat must on no account be allowed to burn in the bottom of the pan, while the turkey is roasting; arrange the damper to be certain to avoid this. The giblets may be put on in a quart of water, which may be allowed to boil down to a pint; then chop them, and add either to the dressing or gravy. — *Commercial Gazette, Cincinnati, O. (By per.)*

Turkey dressed with Oysters.

For a ten-pound turkey, take two pints of bread-crumbs, half a teacupful of butter cut in bits (not melted), one teaspoonful of sweet basil, pepper, and salt, and mix thoroughly. Rub the turkey well, inside and out, with salt and pepper; then fill with first a spoonful of crumbs, then a few well-drained oysters, using half a can for the turkey. Strain the oyster-liquor, and use to baste the turkey. Cook the giblets in the pan, and chop fine in the gravy. A fowl of this size will require three hours cooking in a moderate oven. — PRESBYTERIAN COOK-BOOK, *Dayton, O. Mrs. W. A. B. (By per.)*

Utilizing the "Left-Overs."

The remnants of the turkey, after the best bits have been removed from the bones for other use, make a most delicious soup. Place all the bones and bits of dressing in an earthen vessel, cover with cold water, and simmer for two hours. Remove the bones, and strain the stock through a hair sieve or cloth, to clear away all bits of meat, skin, gristle, or bread-crumbs. Half an hour before straining the stock, prepare two medium-sized bunches of celery by washing, and cutting into pieces an inch long. Use both the leaves and green parts of the stems, as well as the blanched. Put it on the stove in cold water, and when the stock is ready, add both water and celery to it. Season well with salt and whole peppers. Variety may be given by using several kinds of vegetables for flavoring, — cabbage, turnip, onion, and carrot, a very small quantity of each. Instead of vegetables, dumplings made thus may be added: Beat two eggs very light, add half a teaspoonful of salt, same of baking-powder, and flour enough to make a stiff dough; pinch off bits the size of a large hickory-nut, roll between the fingers round, and drop them into the boiling stock half an hour before the soup is to be served. One of the most simple ways of warming up cold turkey is to separate all bits of skin and gristle from the pieces which have been cut from the bones when preparing them for soup, and placing the meat, not chopped, but shred in long pieces, in a frying-pan with sufficient melted butter to fry it. It should be stirred lightly several times, and not fried brown, or it will be too hard. If there is any cold stuffing, cut it in pieces, fry brown after the turkey has been taken up, and place it around the edge of the plate. — *Harper's Bazar.* (*By per. Harper & Brothers.*)

Cranberries.

Put *three pints* of washed *cranberries* in a granite stewpan. On top of them put *three cups* of *granulated sugar* and *three gills* of *water.* After they begin to boil, cook them ten minutes, closely covered, and do *not* stir them. Remove the scum. They will jelly when cool, and the skins will be soft and tender. — THE BOSTON COOK-BOOK : *Mrs. D. A. Lincoln. Roberts Brothers, Pubs.* (*By per.*)

A Chestnut Purée.

Slit the husks of fifty chestnuts, and put them in a saucepan with a bit of butter; put the lid on, and let them heat, tossing the pan now and then. In about twenty minutes you can easily remove all the hulls. Put the nuts in a saucepan with a ladleful of stock, beef-tea, or hot water; let them simmer gently until soft; pound them; put them through a sieve or colander; add a little nutmeg, salt, and sugar; serve up very hot with a dash of cream or butter.

This is for a garnish to chops or cutlets. Serve in a gravy-boat, and then it will keep hot. To put around roast turkey, they are prepared in the same way, but kept whole, and the consommé or beef-tea is cooked down to a glaze and with a little butter, so that they are shiny. Toss them about in it to cover them all over. — *Public Ledger, Philadelphia.* (*By per. Editor of The Household.*)

Such a bustle ensued, that you might have thought a goose the rarest of all birds, a feathered phenomenon to which a black swan was a matter of course; and in truth it was something very like it, in that house. Mrs. Cratchit made the gravy (ready beforehand in a little saucepan) hissing hot; Master Peter mashed the potatoes with incredible vigor; Miss Belinda sweetened up the apple-sauce; Martha dusted the hot plates; Bob took Tiny Tim beside him in a tiny corner at the table; the two young Cratchits set chairs for everybody, not forgetting themselves, and, mounting guard upon their posts, crammed spoons into their mouths, lest they should shriek for goose before their turn came to be helped. At last the dishes were set on, and grace was said. It was succeeded by a breathless pause, as Mrs. Cratchit, looking slowly all along the carving-knife, prepared to plunge it in the breast; but when she did, and when the long-expected gush of stuffing issued forth, one murmur of delight arose all round the board, and even Tiny Tim, excited by the two young Cratchits, beat on the table with the handle of his knife, and feebly cried, Hurrah!

There never was such a goose. Bob said he didn't believe there ever was such a goose cooked. Its tenderness and flavor, size and cheapness, were the themes of universal admiration. Eked out by apple-sauce and mashed potatoes, it was a sufficient dinner for the whole family; indeed, as Mrs. Cratchit said with great delight (surveying one small atom of a bone upon the dish), they hadn't ate it all at last! Yet every one had had enough, and the youngest Cratchits in particular were steeped in sage and onion to the eyebrows! — A CHRISTMAS CAROL: *Charles Dickens.*

To Roast a Goose.

"Take a young goose, pick, singe, and clean well. Make the stuffing with two ounces of onions (about four common-sized) and one ounce of green sage chopped very fine; then add a large coffee-cup of stale bread-crumbs and the same of mashed potatoes, a little pepper and salt, a bit of butter as big as a walnut, the yolk of an egg or two; mix these well together, and then stuff the goose. Do not fill it entirely: the stuffing requires room to swell. It will take two hours or more to roast it thoroughly. The fire must be brisk. Baste it with salt and water at first, then with its own dripping.

"A green goose — that is, one under four months old — is seasoned with pepper and salt instead of sage and onions. It will roast in an hour."

Apple-Sauce for Goose.

Peel, core, and cut up a gallon of pippins or other fresh apples; stew them, with a little water added, grate in a bit of the peel of a lemon and all its juice; sweeten to your taste when the apples are done very tender, mash them up perfectly smooth, and serve. — VIRGINIA COOKERY-BOOK : *Mrs. Mary Stuart Smith. Harper & Brothers, Pubs.* (*By per.*)

Duckling Pot Roast.

This is a very good way to cook this very acceptable bird. Put into a shallow crock a thin strip of bacon and a tablespoonful of mixed whole spice. Clean and truss two ducklings, put them in the crock, add hot water or soup-stock enough to come up half way on the birds. Then add a sprig of celery and two of parsley; place a narrow strip of bacon over each bird; cover close, and set the crock in a moderate oven, where the birds will cook slowly two hours. Remove the ducklings, strain the sauce, and reduce it one-third by boiling; add a gill of dark wine; thicken with a dash of brown flour; simmer fifteen minutes; add a teaspoonful of lemon-juice, and serve with the duck. A small quantity of the sauce may be boiled down until thick as cream. This is called glaze: it is brushed over the bird before serving. — THE BOOK OF ENTRÉES : *Thomas J. Murrey. White, Stokes, & Allen, Pubs.*

The most elegant dish of the Romans was a stuffed peacock. A young peacock is eatable when properly roasted, but an old one is really very poor eating; but the Romans used to prepare them in the following way: They selected those with the most beautiful plumage, and stifled them to death, believing that that mode of killing gave more brilliancy to the plumage. As soon as dead, they carefully split the bird open by an incision all along the back, from the bill to the rump. They then took out all the bones, meat, etc., leaving only the bones of the legs to the first joint, those of the wings to the second joint, and the head whole, except the brain, eyes, and tongue. The inside of the skin was now immediately lined with a coating of glue, and filled with bran to keep it in shape. The feathers that were spoiled were varnished, and false but brilliant eyes were placed instead of the natural ones. When dry the skin was filled with roasted birds or with the flesh of birds chopped and cooked, and carefully sewed up. The bird was served on a large silver dish made for that purpose. The dish was of an oblong shape, and in the middle and soldered to it was something resembling the trunk of a tree with a kind of limb on which the bird was fastened. It was meant to look just as if it were alive, and resting itself on a perch, with an ear of millet in its bill. It was always served at the beginning of the dinner, and was one of the last dishes eaten. — *Pierre Blot.*

Chicken Fricassee.

"Take two chickens, cut up, and lay them in skillet, with two slices of lean ham, two small eschalots, and a few blades of mace. Then season fowls with pepper and salt. Add a little water. When about half done, add half a pint of cream, and a lump of butter the size of a walnut, rolled in flour. Keep the fricassee constantly stirring till done."

A Soufflé of Chicken.

Take the white meat of a chicken, remove all the skin and sinews, and mince it up as fine as possible. Then put the meat into a stew-pan, together with some white sauce, a little parsley chopped fine, and pepper and salt. Set the pan on the fire, and stir it until it boils; then remove it to one side to cool a little. Have the yolks of three eggs beaten to a firm froth, and stir these into the mixture. Butter well a mould, strew over the bottom and sides of it some fine bread-crumbs, and place a piece of white paper around the top to allow the soufflé to rise. Then put it in a very quick oven to bake, and when done, serve with white sauce poured round it. — *The Caterer.* (*By per.*)

Chicken Curry.

Fine-grained poultry does not make good curry, as the curry-powder is unable to permeate the centre of the flesh. A coarse-grained bird will be found the best for this purpose. Boil the chicken in the usual manner, saving the broth. When cold, cut it neatly, and rub the curry-powder into the meat. Cut up one large sour apple and half an onion; fry these in butter; add the meat, toss it about a moment, and add half a pint of the chicken-broth and a tablespoonful of chutney, simmer until thoroughly amalgamated, and serve with rice or shredded maize. A little sugar is an improvement, and may thicken the sauce, but I like it without flour. — THE BOOK OF ENTRÉES: *Thomas J. Murrey. White, Stokes, & Allen, Pubs.*

Chicken Salad. No. 1.

"Mince the white meat of a chicken fine, or pull it in bits; chop the white parts of celery. Prepare a salad-dressing thus: Rub the yolks of four hard-boiled eggs to a smooth paste with a dessertspoonful of salad-oil, two teaspoonfuls of made mustard, one teaspoonful of salt, and one teacupful of strong vinegar. Mix the chicken and celery together, and pour the dressing over when ready to serve. Garnish the dish with the delicate leaves of the celery. White-heart lettuce may be substituted for the celery."

Chicken Salad. No. 2.

"For one good-sized chicken take one bunch of celery chopped fine, a little pepper and salt. For dressing for the above quantity, take the yolks of two eggs boiled hard, make them fine, and add mustard, vinegar, oil, and a little cayenne-pepper and salt to suit taste. The liquor the chicken is boiled in is very nice to use in mixing it. Put in just enough to moisten it nicely. When it becomes cold it is like a jelly, but it is a great improvement to the salad."

Jellied Chicken.

Boil a fowl until it will slip easily from the bones; let the water be reduced to about one pint in boiling; pick the meat from the bones in good-sized pieces, taking out all gristle, fat, and bones; place in a wet mould; skim the fat from the liquor, add a little butter, pepper and salt to the taste, and one half-ounce of gelatine. When this dissolves, pour it hot over the chicken. The liquor must be seasoned pretty high, for the chicken absorbs. — THE EVERY-DAY COOK-BOOK: *Miss E. Neill.* (*By per. Belford, Clarke, & Co.*)

Chicken Pie.

Boil the fowls until tender; prepare a crust of buttermilk and cream, in the same manner as for soft biscuit; line your baking-dish with a portion of it;

then break the fowls in pieces, and place the portions around in the pie. Put in some lumps of butter; then put in the liquid in which the fowls were boiled, until the pan is two-thirds full. It should be seasoned to the taste before putting in, but not have any thickening in, or it will dry away too much. Roll out, and wet the edge where the crust comes together. Make a hole in the top to let out the steam. Bake it moderately. At least two fowls will be necessary for a large pie. — *From Peterson's Magazine. (By per.)*

Chicken Pie with Sweet Potatoes.

Cut up a chicken, and put on to stew; and after it has boiled a while (skimming it when necessary), add six medium-sized sweet potatoes peeled and cut in halves. Stew until tender, and then place the pieces of chicken and potatoes alternately in a large pie-dish lined with crust made as for biscuit. Season with pepper and salt, and the gravy furnished by stewing the chicken and potatoes. Cover with crust, and bake. — *Lizzie Strohm.*

Giblet Pie.

Wash and clean the giblets, put them in a stew-pan, season with pepper, salt, and a little butter rolled in flour; cover them with water, stew them till they are very tender. Line the sides of your pie-dish with paste, put in the giblets, and if the gravy is not quite thick enough, add a little more butter rolled in flour, and let it boil once. Pour in the gravy, put on the top crust, leaving an opening in the centre of it in the form of a square; ornament this with leaves of the paste. Set the pie in the oven, and when the crust is done take it out. — *Peterson's Magazine.* (*By per.*)

Pigeon Pie.

Having picked and cleaned five pigeons, fill them with a stuffing of grated cold ham, grated cracker, salt, pepper, and butter. If asparagus is in season, the green tops may be substituted for the cracker. Pour milk and water into the dish until the pigeons are nearly covered. Put a lid of paste on the top, and bake an hour. If you wish the pigeons very tender, parboil them twenty minutes, and use the water in which they were boiled to make the pie. — *Arthur's Home Magazine.* (*By per. Pubs.*)

<small>The pigeons were snugly put to bed in a comfortable pie, and tucked in with a coverlet of crust. — LEGEND OF SLEEPY HOLLOW: *Washington Irving.* (*By per. G. P. Putnam's Sons.*)</small>

Roast Guinea Fowls.

Pick, clean, wash, and stuff as you would chickens, adding to the stuffing a little minced ham. Roast as you would chickens, basting liberally with butter. Season the gravy with a chopped shallot, and with summer-savory; add the giblets, and thicken with browned flour. — THE UNRIVALLED COOK-BOOK: *Mrs. Washington.* (*By per. Harper & Brothers.*)

Croquettes de Volaille. (Poultry Croquettes.)

Melt a bit of butter in a stew-pan, put into it chopped parsley and mushrooms, two spoonfuls of flour, salt, pepper, and nutmeg. Fry it, and pour in stock and a little cream. This sauce ought to have the consistence of thick milk. Cut up any poultry which has been cooked the day before, into dice. Put them into the sauce, and let it get cold. Form it into balls, and cover them with bread-crumbs. Wash these in eggs which have been beaten up, and roll them in bread-crumbs a second time. Fry them to a good color, and serve with a garnish of fried parsley. — *Peterson's Magazine.* (*By per.*)

CHAPTER VII.

GAME.

GAME.

"I BELIEVE I agree with the English people generally," said Steven, not without a smile. In the levity of youth, ignorance, and unbounded digestion, cooking to him was the least important of subjects. "For myself, a venison steak broiled over a wood fire, a buck's head baked in an earth oven, a partridge or quail quickly roasted, and a snatch of cassava bread, have been my diet for years, with a mug of black coffee — as long as our coffee held out — to wash it down."

A look almost of excitement came across Lord Petres' impassive face. "Lawrence," said he earnestly, "I'm delighted to have met you. Sit down, pray. This conversation is most interesting to me. At the present moment I am endeavoring to work out an idea, — not original, nothing's original, — but an idea too much neglected by writers on art generally; which is, that the perfection of cookery is, in many cases, to be sought, not by striving after new combinations, but by reverting to the instinctive, untaught science of the simple hunter in the woods. Your remark confirms all that I have been writing on the subject. You speak of a venison steak smoking hot from the embers, of small game quickly roasted, of a buck's head cooked by slow and gradual heat. — Good God, sir! do you not know that all this is the *ne plus ultra* of intuitive science, bearing out with accuracy the axiom of the immortal Savarin, that *On devient cuisinier, mais on nait rôtisseur?*"

"I don't know French," said Steven, "except a few words I picked up in the Canadian backwoods once; but I know our food used to taste deuced good to us in the forests or out prairie hunting. Still I can't say I ever enjoyed any thing more than some cold beef and pickles that I ate when I landed in Southampton yesterday. After living on wild flesh, as I have done, for years, I believe plain English beef and mutton will be a treat to me, ill-cooked or well-cooked." — STEVEN LAWRENCE, YEOMAN : *Mrs. Edwards.*

To Cook a Deer's Head in Camp.

Dig a hole two feet square and one foot deep; build a fire in it, and allow it to burn to embers; remove about half of the remaining coals, throw in the hole a thin layer of green leaves, on top of which put the head in the same condition as when taken from the animal; cover it thoroughly with a layer of green leaves, and the embers and ashes previously taken from the hole; allow the head to roast an hour and a half, then remove it, and pull the skin from it; season with salt and pepper. — THE UN-RIVALLED COOK-BOOK: *Mrs. Washington.* (*By per. Harper & Brothers.*)

Venison Steaks, Broiled.

"Wash and wipe them dry. Put them on the gridiron, over a clear fire, and broil them; then season with salt and pepper, and baste them with butter. Serve with currant-jelly."

Venison Steaks, Fried.

"Wash two steaks; season with salt, black and red pepper mixed, and fry a light brown on both sides. When done, place them on a dish, and dredge into the pan one dessertspoonful of browned flour, to which add gradually one cupful of boiling water; stir well, and season to taste. Garnish the top of each with currant-jelly, and send to table on a well-heated dish."

Opossums.

Opossums are best in the autumn when the persimmons are ripe, as they eat that fruit, and become very fat. They are never caught in the daytime. A fine moonlight night is the best time to catch opossums. When caught, put them in a cage, and feed them for several days; skin and draw the opossum, cut off the legs to the first joint, and part of the tail; stuff the head and body like a turkey, and roast it before a brisk fire. Opossums are never eaten hot. — THE UNRIVALLED COOK-BOOK. (*By per Harper & Brothers.*)

> De frosts dun come, an' de 'possum is ripe,
> Oh, Jurangy, ho!
> Better'n any beefsteak, better'n any tripe,
> Oh, Jurangy, ho!
> *Arkansaw Traveller.*

Rabbit Curry.

Select two fine rabbits, cut them into neat pieces; put in an earthen crock a thin slice of bacon, add a few pieces of rabbit, sprinkle over it a little curry-powder, salt, fresh grated cocoanut, and a dozen raisins; put in another layer of rabbit, and season it as the first layer; repeat until the rabbit is all used, and you have also used the juice and meat of one fresh or half a pound of dry cocoanut. Moisten the whole with a mild Catawba or Rhine wine; let this stand twenty-four hours; then place the crock in a pot of water, and let it simmer two hours, keeping it well covered. When done serve it on a flat dish, and serve rice separately. — THE BOOK OF ENTRÉES: *Thomas J. Murrey. White, Stokes, & Allen, Pubs.*

Fricassee of Squirrels.

Put two young squirrels into a pot with two ounces of butter, one or two ounces of ham, some salt and pepper, and just water enough to cover them. Let them stew slowly until tender; take them up, and pour half a teacup of cream and a beaten yolk of egg into the gravy, and when it has boiled five minutes, pour over the squirrels in the dish. — *Arthur's Home Magazine.* (*By per.*)

Broiled Partridges.

"Time, fifteen to twenty minutes. Partridges, gravy, butter, pepper, salt, cayenne.

"Thoroughly pick and draw the partridges, divide each through the back and breast, and wipe the insides. Season them highly with pepper, salt, and a very little cayenne, and place them over a clear bright fire to broil. When done, rub a piece of fresh butter over them, and serve them up hot with brown gravy."

Fillet of Grouse.

Remove the breast, and separate into four or six pieces. Disjoint and cook the remainder in boiling salted water to cover, till tender; then remove all the meat, and chop it fine. Thicken the broth (which should be reduced to half a cup), season, and moisten the meat. Spread the minced meat on squares of toast; put a layer of currant-jelly on each. Rub the fillets with butter, and broil them carefully; season with salt, pepper, and butter, and lay them on the jelly. — THE PEERLESS COOK-BOOK: *Mrs. D. A. Lincoln.* (*By per.*)

Woodcock Pie.

Have a good puff-paste made, and with this line the sides of your baking-dish. Then have cut a thin slice of veal; lay this on the bottom of the dish, and season it with salt, pepper, and a little mace, laying upon the top of it a thin slice of ham. (The ham, as well as the veal, should have no fat about it.) Now take a couple of brace of woodcock that have been carefully plucked, and, without drawing, season them with pepper, salt, and mace. Have some bacon cut into thin slices, wrap these round the birds, and lay them on the ham as closely together as possible, filling up the spaces around them with hard-boiled eggs cut in small pieces. Have ready made some very strong beef-gravy; pour a pint of it over the birds, lay over the whole a covering of the puff-paste, brush it over with egg, and bake for three-quarters of an hour in a well-heated oven. This pie is intended to be eaten cold. — *The Caterer.* (*By per.*)

To roast Wild Ducks.

Clean and prepare them as poultry. Crumb the inside of a small loaf of baker's bread, to which add three ounces of butter, one large onion chopped fine, with pepper and salt to taste. Mix all well together. Season the ducks, both inside and out, with pepper, salt, and a little sage rubbed fine; then fill them with the dressing, and skewer tightly. Place them in the pan, back upward; dredge a little flour over, and a tablespoonful in the pan, with water sufficient to make gravy. When a nice brown, turn them over; baste frequently. Serve with currant-jelly. — *Arthur's Home Magazine.* (*By per.*)

CHAPTER VIII.

OMELETS, EGGS, AND CHEESE.

OMELETS, EGGS, AND CHEESE.

FRANCIS. What can you give us for luncheon?
MANETTE. Whatever you are pleased to choose; but, unluckily, we have neither beef, veal, nor mutton in the house.
SERGEANT AUSTERLITZ. Well, well, we are not particular; you have only to twist the neck of one of your fine fat barn-door fowls, and clap it on the gridiron.
MANETTE. Why, as to our fowls, gentlemen, I can't say much for our fowls; our fowls are apt to be tough; but what say you to some fine, fresh, new-laid eggs? If eggs would serve your turn, I could make you out the prettiest bill of fare!
SERGEANT AUSTERLITZ. Your larder does not seem likely to burst from an overcharge, bright tulip of the Seine! . . . Toss us up an omelet, and we will make the best of your fare. — THE MAID OF CROISSEY: *Mrs. Gore.*

Omelette aux Fines Herbes.

"Break eight eggs in a stew-pan, to which add a teaspoonful of very finely chopped eschalots, one of chopped parsley, a half-one of salt, a pinch of pepper, and three large tablespoonfuls of cream; beat them well together; then put two ounces of butter in an omelet-pan, stand it over a sharp fire, and as soon as the butter is sufficiently hot pour in the eggs; stir them round quickly until delicately set; shake the pan round, then leave it a moment to color the omelet; hold the pan in a slanting position, turn it on to your dish, and serve it immediately. It must not be too much done."

Omelette au Sucre.

Break four eggs in a bowl; beat them with a fork for half a minute; add a tablespoonful of sugar;

beat another half-minute. Put a teaspoonful of butter in a frying-pan over a quick fire, and when melted, turn the eggs in; stir with a fork, and see that it does not burn. When becoming hard, — or rather, when the under part is cooked, but the top rather liquid yet, — slide it over the dish, and when about half of it is on the dish, turn the pan upside down so as to fold the omelet over into the form of a semicircle; then dust it with sugar. Have a red-hot poker, or other piece of iron, with which just touch the omelet in spots, so as to make an ornamental design, burning each place slightly, and serve. The whole process must be completed in about three minutes: the quicker, the better the omelet. — *Pierre Blot.*

Omelet with Jelly.

Put a small quantity of lard or oil into the pan, let it simmer a few minutes, and remove it; wipe the pan dry with a towel, and put in a little fresh oil in which the omelet may be fried; care should be taken that the oil does not burn, which would spoil the color of the omelet. Break three eggs separately; put them into a bowl, and whisk them thoroughly with a fork. The longer they are beaten, the lighter will the omelet be. Beat up a teaspoonful of milk with the eggs, and continue to beat until the last moment before pouring into the pan, which should be over a hot fire. As soon as the omelet sets, remove the pan from the hottest part of the fire. Slip a knife under it to prevent sticking to the pan. When the centre is almost firm, slant the pan, work the omelet in shape to fold; just before folding add a teaspoonful of currant-jelly; turn it out on a hot dish, dust a little powdered sugar over it, and serve. This recipe is from "The Cook," and has been amply tested. (*By per.*)

Omelet au Rhum.

Prepare an omelet as has been directed, fold it, and turn out on a hot dish; dust a liberal quantity of powdered sugar over it, and singe the sugar into neat stripes with a hot iron rod heated on the coals. Pour a wineglassful of warmed Jamaica rum around it, and when on the table set fire to it; with a tablespoon dash the burning rum over the omelet; blow out the fire, and serve. — BREAKFAST DAINTIES: *Thomas J. Murrey. White, Stokes, & Allen, Pubs.*

Bread Omelet.

One cup of fine bread-crumbs moistened with half a cup of sweet milk; three eggs beaten separately and thoroughly, adding the whites last; season with salt and pepper to taste. Put in the skillet or frying-pan a good piece of butter, and when hot, pour in the omelet. Leave on the stove a short time, and then finish cooking in a warm oven. — *Mrs. Matilda J. Anderson.*

Plain Omelet.

Break four eggs into a large bowl; beat them thoroughly; season with salt and pepper; take a tablespoonful of flour, and mix very smoothly in a *small* teacupful of sweet milk, then pour it into the bowl with the eggs, and beat all well; have ready a skillet very hot, with a good lump of butter melted in it. Pour in the omelet, and as soon as it becomes "set" in the middle, turn very carefully. Serve hot.

Ham Omelet.

"Two eggs, four ounces of butter, half a salt-spoonful of pepper, two tablespoonfuls of minced ham. Mince the ham very finely, without any fat, and fry it for two minutes in a little butter; then make the batter for the omelet, stir in the ham, and proceed as in the case of a plain omelet. Do not add any salt to the batter, as the ham is usually sufficiently salt to impart a flavor."

Asparagus Omelet.

"Boil some tender fresh-cut asparagus in very little water with a small portion of salt; or, what is better still, steam the asparagus without water until it is tender; chop it very fine, mix it with the yolks of five and whites of three well-beaten eggs; add two tablespoonfuls of sweet cream; fry, and serve quite hot."

Spanish Omelet.

Chop up half of a sweet Spanish pepper; peel and cut up a large tomato; cut two ounces of ham into dice; mince three button mushrooms and half an onion with a clove of garlic; season with salt, cayenne, and capers. Put the onion and ham in a pan, and fry; add the other ingredients, and simmer until a thick pulp; add to this an omelet just before folding it, and turning out on a dish. Pour a well-made tomato-sauce round it, and serve.

The ingredients may be varied to suit the taste. — BREAKFAST DAINTIES: *Thomas J. Murrey. White, Stokes, & Allen, Pubs.*

Omelet Fritters.

Make two or three thin omelets, adding a little sweet basil to the usual ingredients; cut them into small pieces, and roll them into the shape of olives; when cold, dip them into batter, or enclose them into puff-paste, fry, and serve them with fried parsley. — AMERICAN HOME COOK-BOOK. *Dick & Fitzgerald, Pubs.*

Soft-boiled Eggs.

Put the eggs in a warm saucepan, and cover with boiling water. Let them stand where they will keep hot, but *not* boil, for ten minutes. This method will cook both whites and yolks. — NEW COOK-BOOK: *Miss Parloa. Estes & Lauriat, Pubs.* (*By per.*)

There is always a best way of doing every thing, if it be to boil an egg. — *R. W. Emerson.*

Scrambled Eggs.

Four eggs, one tablespoonful of butter, half a teaspoonful of salt. Beat the eggs, and add the salt to them. Melt the butter in a saucepan. Turn in the beaten eggs, stir quickly over a hot fire for one minute, and serve.

Fricasseed Eggs.

Boil half a dozen eggs hard, and cut them into slices. Then make a sauce as follows: Chop very fine a small onion, a little parsley, and two or three mushrooms, and put them into a stew-pan with two ounces of butter, seasoning with salt and pepper. Let them stew gently, but do not brown them. Then add a gill of cream mixed with a little flour, for thickening the sauce, lay the sliced eggs in, allow all to come to a boil, and serve. — *The Caterer.* (*By per.*)

Frothed Eggs.

Take the yolks of eight eggs and the whites of four, and beat them up with a tablespoonful of water and the strained juice of one lemon. Sweeten it to taste, add a pinch of salt, and then fry the same as an omelet. Have ready the four remaining whites whipped to a stiff froth with a pound of pulverized sugar, and flavored with vanilla or lemon. Then dish the omelet, heap the frothed egg high upon it, and put it in the oven for a few minutes to brown. — *The Caterer.* (*By per.*)

Cheese Fritters.

"Three ounces of flour, one egg, one gill of tepid water, three ounces of grated cheese, a little pepper and salt, and one ounce of butter. The flour and condiments are put into a basin, and the water added by degrees. Then the cheese with the yolk of the egg is added, and last the white beaten to a stiff froth. Drop this by spoonfuls into boiling lard, and cook three minutes. The results are delicious golden-brown balls, as big as your fist, permeated with the flavor of the cheese."

Welsh Rarebit.

Grate one pint of cheese; sprinkle on it half a teaspoonful of mustard, one-fourth of a teaspoonful of salt, and a speck of cayenne. Heap this on slices of buttered toast. Put in the hot oven for a few moments, and when the cheese begins to melt, serve at once. — NEW COOK-BOOK: *Miss Parloa. Estes & Lauriat, Pubs. (By per.)*

> The dairy was certainly worth looking at; it was a scene to sicken for with a sort of calenture in hot and dusty streets, — such coolness, such purity, such fresh fragrance of new-pressed cheese, of firm butter, of wooden vessels perpetually bathed in pure water; such soft coloring of red earthenware and creamy surfaces, brown wood and polished tin, gray limestone and rich orange-red rust on the iron weights and hooks and hinges. But one gets only a confused notion of these details when they surround a distractingly pretty girl of seventeen, standing on her little pattens, and rounding her dimpled arm to lift a pound of butter out of the scale. — ADAM BEDE: *George Eliot.*

Curds and Cream.

One gallon of milk will make a moderate dish. Put one spoonful of prepared rennet to each quart of milk, and when you find that it has become curd, tie it loosely in a thin cloth, and hang it to drain; do not wring or press the cloth; when drained, put the curd into a mug, and set in cool water, which must be frequently changed. (A refrigerator saves this trouble.) When you dish it, if there is whey in the mug, ladle it gently out without pressing the curd; lay it on a deep dish, and pour fresh cream over it; have powdered loaf-sugar to eat with it; also hand the nutmeg-grater. — VIRGINIA COOKERY-BOOK: *Mrs. Mary Stuart Smith. Harper & Brothers, Pubs. (By per.)*

Cottage Cheese.

Take two quarts of clabbered milk, and heat on the stove until the curd separates from the whey. (Be careful not to *cook* it.) Place it to drain in a thin muslin bag for six or eight hours, then take it out, put in a dish, and dress it with half a pint of cream, and salt and pepper to taste. — *Lulie Strohm.*

CHAPTER IX.

VEGETABLES AND SALADS.

VEGETABLES AND SALADS.

> Glittering in the freshened fields,
> The snowy mushroom springs.
> *Campbell.*

Mushrooms, Stewed.

If fresh, let them lie in salt and water about one hour, then put them in the stew-pan, cover with water, and stew gently until tender. Dress them with cream, butter, and flour, as oysters, and season to taste.

Fried Mushrooms.

Split, and wash carefully; roll them in flour; season with salt and pepper, and fry them in butter. — *Lizzie Strohm.*

Spinach and other Greens.

"Take *spinach, beet, or turnip tops, poke-sprouts, curled dock, lamb's-quarters,* etc., and wash thoroughly. Put into just enough salted boiling water to cover. When tender, squeeze out all the water, and press through a colander. Fry a few minutes with a little salt, pepper, and butter. Serve with slices of hard-boiled egg."

Water-Cresses.

Wash well, pick off decayed leaves, and leave in ice-water until you are ready to eat them. They should then be shaken free of wet, and piled lightly in a glass dish. Eat with salt. — *Marion Harland. The Post, Washington, D.C.* (*By per.*)

Dandelion Salad.

One pint of the plants are carefully washed, and placed in a salad-bowl with an equal quantity of water-cresses, three green onions or leeks sliced, a teaspoonful of salt, and plenty of oil or cream dressing. This is one of the most healthful and refreshing of all early salads. — COOKING MANUAL: *Miss Juliet Corson. Dodd, Mead, & Co., Pubs.* (*By per.*)

Mayonnaise.

When preparing a mayonnaise in summer, keep the bowl as cold as possible. Beat up the yolks of two raw eggs to a smooth consistency; add two salt-spoonfuls of salt and one of white pepper, and a tablespoonful of oil. Beat up thoroughly, and by degrees add half a pint of oil. When it begins to thicken, add a few drops of vinegar. The total amount of vinegar to be used is two tablespoonfuls; and the proper time to stop adding oil, and to add drops of vinegar, is when the dressing has a glassy look, instead of a velvet appearance. After a few trials, almost any one can make a mayonnaise, as it is very simple. — FIFTY SALADS: *Thomas J. Murrey. White, Stokes, & Allen, Pubs.*

Cream Dressing.

Where oil is disliked in salads, the following dressing will be found excellent. Rub the yolks of two hard-boiled eggs very fine with a spoon, incorporate with them a dessertspoonful of mixed mustard, then stir in a tablespoonful of melted butter, half a teacupful of thick cream, a salt-spoonful of salt, and cayenne-pepper enough to take up on the point of a very small penknife blade, and a few drops of anchovy or Worcestershire sauce; add very carefully sufficient vinegar to reduce the mixture to a smooth, creamy consistency. — COOKING MANUAL : *Miss Corson. Dodd, Mead, & Co., Pubs.* (*By per.*)

Lettuce Salad.

"Take two large lettuces, pull off the outer leaves, and throw them away; take off the others one by one, and cut in two, and wash thoroughly. Cut them up, and put in a bowl; sprinkle over a teaspoonful of salt, half a one of pepper, add three of oil and two of vinegar, and with a spoon and fork turn the salad lightly in the bowl till well mixed; the less it is handled, the better. Garnish with hard-boiled eggs sliced. The flower of the nasturtium, intermixed with taste and care, improves the appearance of the salad."

Mustard and Cress.

"These, if eaten alone, make an excellent salad. Wash quickly, and dress as lettuce."

Radishes.

Radishes should always be freshly gathered. Let them be in cold water one hour before serving, then cut off all their leaves and almost all their stalk. Serve them in glasses half filled with water, or on a plate. — *Arthur's Home Magazine.* (*By per.*)

Cucumbers.

"Let them be as fresh as possible, or they will be unwholesome. Pare, cut off the stem end to the seeds, and slice in cold water some time before they are wanted. Season well with salt, pepper, and vinegar. Onions are frequently sliced with them, and are an improvement."

Melons.

All varieties of the cantelope family, musk and nutmeg melons, are welcome to the summer breakfast-table. Cut each in half lengthwise; scoop out the seeds, put a lump of ice in the hollows thus made, and send to table. They are eaten by Southerners with pepper and salt; at the North, with sugar. Give your guests their choice of condiments. — *Marion Harland. The Post, Washington, D.C.*

To cook Asparagus.

Asparagus must be carefully washed and cleaned, and all the tough parts cut off. Put into salted boiling water, and boil until tender. Arrange upon thin slices of buttered toast, put some melted butter over them, and a little of the liquor in which they were stewed. Set in the oven for a few minutes.

I stick to asparagus, which still seems to inspire gentle thoughts. GRACE BEFORE MEAT: *Charles Lamb.*

Green Peas stewed with Ham and Lettuce.

Put a quart of young peas into a bowl of cold water, with a piece of butter the size of an egg. Work the butter and the peas well together without mashing them, and then drain them, and put them into a stew-pan, adding the hearts of two heads of lettuce finely shredded, an onion cut into thin slices, a little parsley, and half a pound of ham cut into dice. Now cover the stew-pan, and place it over a gentle fire, where the contents may stew, shaking the stew-pan occasionally that they may not burn, and adding a spoonful or two of water if necessary. When the peas become tender, take out the ham and the onion; mix a dessertspoonful of flour with a little butter and a tablespoonful of cream, and stir this into the peas. Simmer them again gently for three or four minutes, and serve hot. — *The Caterer*. (*By per.*)

Green Peas.

Shell and wash, put them into cold water to cook; when nearly done, salt them; when tender (they will generally cook in twenty minutes) take them up with a little of the liquor in which they were boiled, butter and pepper them, and they are much better to add a little sweet cream, but will do without. If they are cooked immediately upon gathering, they will need no sugar; if allowed to remain twelve hours or more, a tablespoonful of sugar will be found an addition. A sprig of mint or a little parsley may be added. — *Arthur's Home Magazine*. (*By per.*)

> And the maize-field grew and ripened,
> Till it stood in all the splendor
> Of its garments green and yellow,
> Of its tassels and its plumage;
> And the maize-ears full and shining
> Gleamed from bursting sheaves of verdure.

HIAWATHA: *H. W. Longfellow*. (*By per. Houghton, Mifflin, & Co.*)

Sweet Corn.

Husk and clear it of the silk, put it in boiling water enough to cover, and boil for twenty minutes or half an hour. Send to table on the cob. — *Arthur's Home Magazine.*

ANOTHER WAY.

Cut the corn from the cob, and put it in a stew-pan with a teacupful of water to each quart of corn; cover it closely, and let it stew gently. Add butter, pepper, and salt. — *Arthur's Home Magazine.*

Still another excellent way is to prepare and season corn as above, but stew it in sweet milk instead of water. Have sufficient milk to cover it well.

Corn Oysters.

"Take young green corn, grate in a dish; to one pint of this add a small teacupful of flour, one egg, half a cup of butter, some salt and pepper, and mix well. Fry in butter. Drop by the spoonful, the size of an oyster."

Succotash.

"Common shelled beans may be used for succotash, though Lima beans are the best. Prepare and cook the beans as usual. About twenty minutes before serving, add a quantity of sweet corn cut from the cob; season with butter, pepper, and salt, and add a little sweet cream. This dish may be prepared with pork if desirable."

String Beans.

String, snap, and wash two quarts beans, boil in plenty of water fifteen minutes, drain off, and put on again in two quarts boiling water; boil an hour and a half, and add salt and pepper just before taking up, stirring in one and a half tablespoonfuls butter rubbed into two tablespoonfuls flour and a half-pint sweet cream.

ANOTHER WAY.

Boil a piece of salted pork one hour, then add beans, and boil an hour and a half. — EVERY-DAY COOK-BOOK: *Miss Neill.* (*By per. Belford, Clarke, & Co.*)

Lentils Boiled plain.

Wash one pound, or one full pint, of lentils (cost ten cents) well in cold water, put them over the fire in three quarts of cold water, with one ounce of drippings, one tablespoonful of salt, and a saltspoonful of pepper (cost about one cent), and boil slowly until tender, that is, about three hours; drain off the little water which remains; add to the lentils one ounce of butter, a tablespoonful of chopped parsley, a teaspoonful of sugar, and a little more salt and pepper if required (cost about three cents), and serve them hot. — TWENTY-FIVE-CENT DINNERS: *Miss Juliet Corson. O. Judd Co., Pubs.* (*By per.*)

Mashed Potato.

There is no dish which is capable of being made into a delicious one, that is so often set before us in an unpalatable, unsavory condition, as the apparently simple one of mashed potato. It may be light unto flakiness, white, and with a dry creaminess that melts in the mouth; or it may be a heavy, sodden, packed-down mass, strongly flavored by the old iron pot.

To insure the former composition, the potatoes

should be put on in boiling water, and allowed from twenty to twenty-five minutes for cooking; test them at the end of twenty minutes, and if the fork will go into them at all, take them right off. Do not wait until they are so soft that the piercing of a fork will tear them to pieces. Pour every drop of water off, set them back on the stove, with the lid off one or two minutes to allow the steam to pass off, and then, with a wire beater, begin the mashing process, salting according to the taste of the family. To a half-gallon of peeled potatoes, a teaspoon rounded over with salt and a heaping tablespoonful of butter is sufficient. When the lumps are thoroughly beaten out, add a half-pint, or even a little less, of hot milk, and then whip and beat until your arm aches badly. Put them into a heated dish, but do not press, pat, or smooth them down, and serve immediately. — *Commercial Gazette, Cincinnati, O.* (*By per.*)

Potato Hillocks.

Whip boiled potatoes light with a little butter and milk, and season with salt and pepper. Beat in a raw egg to bind the mixture; shape into small conical heaps, set in a greased pan in the oven, and as they brown glare with butter. The oven must be very hot. Slip a cake-turner under each hillock, and transfer to a hot platter. — *Marion Harland: The Post, Washington, D.C.* (*By per.*)

Potatoes au Maitre d'hôtel.

"Cut cold boiled potatoes into quarter-inch slices, and put into a saucepan with four or five tablespoonfuls of milk, two of butter, some pepper and salt and chopped parsley. Heat quickly, stirring all the time until ready to boil, when stir in the juice of half a lemon. Serve very hot."

Saratoga Potatoes.

Take four large potatoes (new ones are best); pare, and cut into thin slices on a slaw-cutter; put them into salt water, and let stand while breakfast is preparing. Then have ready a skillet of boiling lard. Take a handful of the potatoes, squeeze the water from them, and dry in a napkin; separate the slices, and drop into the lard, being careful that the pieces do not adhere to each other. Stir with a fork till they are a light brown color. Take them out with a wire spoon, and drain well before putting into the dish. Do not put more than a handful into the lard at a time. Do not cover the dish when served. — PRESBYTERIAN COOK-BOOK: *Mrs. D. W. S., Dayton, O.* (*By per.*)

Potato Scones.

"Mash boiled potatoes till they are quite smooth, adding a little salt; then knead out with flour to the thickness required; toast, pricking them with a fork to prevent their blistering. When eaten with fresh butter, they are very nutritious."

Potato Stew.

Wash and pare three or four good-sized potatoes, and cut them into small pieces; boil until tender; then drain off the water, and put in three pints of sweet milk; when it begins to boil, add two cupfuls of nice wheat bread crumbed (not too small); season with salt, pepper, and butter.

Potato Salad.

Cut up into slices two quarts of boiled potatoes *while hot;* add to them a teaspoonful each of chopped onion and parsley; pour over them a liberal quantity of plain salad-dressing. If the potatoes should then appear too dry, add a little hot water, or, better still, soup-stock; toss lightly so as not to break the slices; then place the salad on ice to become cold. Serve by placing a leaf of lettuce on each small plate, and add two tablespoonfuls of the potato to the lettuce, for each person. Cold boiled potatoes do not make a good potato-salad. — FIFTY SALADS: *Thomas J. Murrey. White, Stokes, & Allen, Pubs.*

To Boil Sweet Potatoes.

Wash them perfectly clean, put them into a pot or stew-pan, and pour boiling water over to cover them; cover the pot close, and boil fast for half an hour, or more if the potatoes are large; try them with a fork; when done, drain off the water, take off the skins, and serve.

Cold sweet potatoes may be cut in slices across or lengthwise, and fried or broiled as common potatoes. — THE EVERY-DAY COOK-BOOK: *Miss Neill.*

Society expects every man to have certain things in his garden. Not to raise cabbage, is as if one had no pew in church. Perhaps we shall come some day to free churches and free gardens; when I can show my neighbor through my tired garden, at the end of the season, when skies are overcast, and brown leaves are swirling down, and not mind if he does raise his eyebrows when he observes, "Ah! I see you have none of this, and of that." At present we want the moral courage to plant only what we need; to spend only what will bring us peace, regardless of what is going on over the fence. — MY SUMMER IN A GARDEN: *Chas. D. Warner.* Houghton, Mifflin, & Co., Pubs. (*By per.*)

Boiled Cabbage.

Cut the cabbage in quarters, and wash very thoroughly in cold water. Put it into a pot in which a good piece of beef or pork has already been boiling for half an hour and been well skimmed. Boil until the cabbage is tender, and a little before dishing out put in one-fourth of a teaspoonful of soda.

To Stew Cabbage à la Cauliflower.

Parboil in milk and water, and drain it, then shred it, put it into a stew-pan with a small piece of butter, a small teacupful of cream, and seasoning, and stew tender. — *Peterson's Magazine.* (*By per.*)

Red Cabbage Stewed.

After slicing a small red cabbage, and well washing it, put it into a saucepan with pepper, salt, and butter, but no more water than will hang about it after the washing. Let it stew until quite tender, and shortly before serving add two or three spoonfuls of vinegar, and give it one boil over the fire. It may be sent up with cold meat, or with sausages on it. — *Godey's Lady's Book.* (*By per.*)

Cream Dressing for Cold Slaw.

In a small granite stewer beat the yolk of one egg (this for a pint of finely shaved cabbage), add a piece of butter the size of a nutmeg, two teaspoonfuls of sugar, half a teaspoonful of salt, a sprinkle of pepper, half a teacupful each of vinegar and water; put on the back of the stove to simmer, and stir in a scant teaspoonful of flour made smooth with water; when boiled, pour over the cabbage. This is a favorite dressing. — *Commercial Gazette, Cincinnati, O.* (*By per.*)

Stewed Tomatoes.

Peel and slice a quart of fine ripe tomatoes. Put on to stew, and when nearly done add a good-sized lump of butter, a little salt and pepper, two teaspoonfuls of sugar, and half a teacupful of stale bread-crumbs. Cook well and thoroughly, stirring often.

Broiled Tomatoes.

"Large solid tomatoes are cut in halves crosswise, placed on a gridiron or broiler, and put over a brisk fire, cut surface down. In eight or ten minutes, according to size, turn, put upon each half salt, pepper, and a lump of butter, and cook with the skin-side down, rather more slowly than before, about as long, or until done. When sufficiently broiled, place upon a platter with the cut side up, and nicely butter the surface. This gives a proper seasoning to the dish, which is now ready for the breakfast-table."

Tomatoes au Gratin.

This simple and delicious dish is made by cutting some ripe tomatoes in half, putting them in a buttered dish with bread-crumbs, butter, pepper, and salt, and baking till slightly browned on the top. — *Arthur's Home Magazine.* (*By per.*)

I doubt not that all men and women love the onion; but few confess their love. Affection for it is concealed. Good New-Englanders are as shy of owning it as they are of talking about religion. Some people have days on which they eat onions — what you might call "retreats," or their "Thursdays." — MY SUMMER IN A GARDEN: *Chas. D. Warner.* (*By per.*)

Boiled Onions.

Wash the onions well, and peel, and if *large* cut in half. Boil in several waters, draining well each time; and when done, add for seasoning, butter, cream or rich milk, and salt and pepper. Cook a few minutes after seasoning is added.

Baked Onions.

Boil the onions slightly in water; cut in halves, and take out the centres. Fill the cups with a stuffing of bread-crumbs moistened with an egg and a little butter; season with grated cheese, pepper, and thyme. Bake in a quick oven, with a little gravy to prevent from burning. — *Boston Bulletin.*

Turnips à la Poulette.

Cut the turnips in dice, and put in a saucepan. When boiled tender, turn them into a colander. Put a little butter and flour in a saucepan, and stir. Add a gill of milk, and stir, then the turnips, and salt and pepper to taste. — *Peterson's Magazine.*

To Stew Celery.

"Wash well, and cut into lengths of three or four inches; stew them with a little broth until tender; then add two spoonfuls of cream, and some floured butter seasoned with salt and pepper, and simmer all together."

<blockquote>
Such vegetables as celery ought to lengthen human life, at least, to correct its biliousness, and make it more sweet and sanguine. — LOCUSTS AND WILD HONEY: *John Burroughs. Houghton, Mifflin, & Co., Pubs. (By per.)*
</blockquote>

Beets.

Clean these nicely, but do not pare them, leaving on a short piece of the stalk. Then put on to boil in hot water. Young beets will cook tender in an hour; old beets require several hours' boiling. When done, skin quickly while hot, slice thin into your vegetable-dish, put on salt, pepper, and a little butter, put over a little vinegar, and serve hot or cold. — THE EVERY-DAY COOK-BOOK: *Miss Neill. Belford, Clarke, & Co., Pubs. (By per.)*

Parsnip Fritters.

Boil four or five parsnips; when tender, take off the skin and mash them fine; add to them a teaspoonful of wheat flour and a beaten egg. Put a tablespoonful of lard or beef-dripping in a frying-pan over the fire, add to it a saltspoonful of salt; when boiling hot, put in the parsnips, making them in small cakes with a spoon; when one side is a delicate brown, turn the other; when both are done, take them on a dish, put a very little of the fat in which they were fried over, and serve hot. These resemble very nearly the taste of the salsify or oyster-plant. — THE EVERY-DAY COOK-BOOK: *Miss Neill. Belford, Clarke, & Co., Pubs.*

Squashes.

"Cut them up, and remove the seeds, and cook in hot water until tender. Then mash them, and dress with butter, salt, and pepper."

Egg-Plant.

Cut the plant into slices one-third of an inch thick, without removing the skin. Sprinkle salt over each slice, pile them, and cover with a weight to press out the juice. Drain, and dip each slice first in fine crumbs, then in beaten egg, and again in crumbs, and sauté them in hot fat. — THE PEERLESS COOK-BOOK: *Mrs. D. A. Lincoln.* (*By per.*)

Rice, Japanese Style.

Put half a pound of well-washed rice into a double kettle, with one pint of milk or water, one heaping teaspoonful of salt, and quarter of a medium-sized nutmeg grated; boil it until tender, about forty minutes; if it seems very dry, add a little more liquid, taking care not to have it sloppy when it is cooked. When milk is used, it may be served with milk and sugar as a breakfast or tea dish; when water takes the place of milk, the addition of an ounce of butter and half a saltspoonful of pepper makes a nice dinner dish of it. — TWENTY-FIVE-CENT DINNERS: *Miss Juliet Corson.* (*By per.*)

Baked Macaroni.

Boil half a pound of macaroni until quite soft; put it into a vegetable-dish, with a little mustard, pepper, and salt, a small piece of butter, and some grated cheese. Bake ten or fifteen minutes. — PRESBYTERIAN COOK-BOOK. (*By per.*)

CHAPTER X.

PICKLES.

PICKLES.

Pickled Cucumbers.

Take small cucumbers, wash them carefully, and let them drain, then pack them in a jar. Make a brine of a pint of salt to a gallon and a half of water; boil and skim it, and when cool pour over the pickles, and let them stand for twenty-four hours. Then take them out of the brine, wipe them dry, and put in a jar. Boil strong vinegar with such spices as desired (tie the spices in a little cloth), and when the vinegar is cold pour it over the pickles. In a few days they will be ready for use. — *Miss Lizzie Strohm.*

To Pickle Ripe Cucumbers.

Pare them, take out the seeds, cut in rings an inch thick, then simmer in weak alum-water an hour; take them out, drain them, and lay them carefully in a jar. Then prepare a sirup of one gallon good vinegar, two cups sugar, one ounce cinnamon, and one ounce ginger-root; pour it hot over your pickles. This is a delightful pickle, and will keep, sealed up, a long time. — *Godey's Lady's Book.* (*By per.*)

Pickled Onions.

Take small white onions, and peel them; lay them in salt water for two days; change the water once, then drain them in a cloth, and put them in bottles.

Boil mace, pepper, and vinegar together; let it cool, and pour over the pickles. — PRESBYTERIAN COOK-BOOK, *Dayton, O.* (*By per.*)

Green Tomato Pickles.

"A peck of green tomatoes, sliced; one dozen onions, sliced also; sprinkle them with salt, and let them stand until the next day, when drain them. Then use the following as spices: one box of mustard, one and a half ounces of black pepper, one ounce of whole cloves, one ounce of yellow mustard-seed, one ounce of allspice. Put in the kettle a layer of spices, and one of tomatoes and onions, alternately. Cover them with vinegar: wet the mustard before putting it in. Let the whole boil twenty minutes, and you will have pickles so good that you will be pestered by all your friends asking you for the recipe."

Piccalilly.

Take green tomatoes, chopped very fine; sprinkle well with salt, let stand twenty-four hours, drain off, and put in a stone jar. Take about half the quantity of cucumbers, and the same of cabbage; after they are chopped, put into jars separately, and cover with cold vinegar. Take about one-quarter as much white onions chopped; salt, and pour boiling water on them; let stand a few hours, drain off, and cover with vinegar as above. Let all remain several days in a cool place, then press very dry, and mix together. Add some yellow and black mustard-seed, celery-seed, and a bountiful supply of grated horseradish, with a few green peppers chopped fine. Then take the best vinegar, and about four pounds of brown sugar to each gallon. Boil it in part of the vinegar, skim well, and pour over the whole. Add as much cold vinegar as is required. — PRESBYTERIAN COOK-BOOK : *Mrs. J. F. Edgar.*

Mango.

"A green muskmelon, stuffed and pickled." — *Worcester.*

Take an unripe muskmelon, just before they begin to ripen the better, wash it in cold water; cut out a small section on the side most rounded, and scoop out the seeds and soft pulp; scrape off the soft matter from the section, and preserve it for the "lid." Pare off the rind carefully, so as to leave all of the tender portion of the shell. Put a tablespoonful of salt in the cavity, place it in a bowl, and pour hot water in and over it, and let it remain eight to twelve hours. Then have your filling, — generally of finely chopped cabbage, but it is a matter of taste. Beet-stems, tender string-beans, radish seed-pods, etc., can be used. Three or four small slices of green pepper, lining the shell, will spice it; white mustard-seed, or any other condiment, is good. A preferable way is to tie up in a small piece of muslin the spices you desire, and boil them in the vinegar in which you pickle it.

The hot water and salt make the shell soft and pliable, and render the "stuffing" process easy. When filled, stitch the segment cut out of it carefully over the aperture.

A common practice is to "disembowel" a large red or green pepper, and fill it with the chopped vegetable. But the advantage in the melon is, that the rind is better than the best cucumber pickle. — *I. S.* "*The Elms,*" *near Dayton, O.*

To Pickle Beet-root.

This vegetable makes an excellent pickle, and from the brightness of its color has a very pretty effect in a glass pickle-dish or jar. Wash the beet perfectly; do not cut off any of the fibrous roots, as this would allow the juice to escape, and thus the coloring would be lost. Put it into sufficient water to boil it, and when the skin will come off it will be sufficiently cooked, and may be taken out and laid upon a cloth to cool. Having rubbed off the skin, cut the beet into thick slices, put it into a jar, and pour over it cold vinegar prepared as follows: Boil a quart of vinegar with one ounce of whole black pepper and an equal weight of dry ginger, and let it stand until quite cold. The jar should be kept closely corked. — *Peterson's Magazine.* (*By per.*)

To Pickle Carrot.

"Boil carrots until tender, cut them in fancy shapes, and put them in strong vinegar. This is a pretty garnish and an excellent pickle. It can be spiced or flavored to suit the taste."

To Pickle Red Cabbage.

Cut the cabbage across in very thin slices, lay it on a large dish, sprinkle a good handful of salt over it, and cover it with another dish; let it stand twenty-four hours; put it in a colander to drain, and then lay it in the jar. Take white-wine vinegar sufficient to cover it, a little mace, cloves, and allspice, and put them in whole, with one pennyworth of cochineal bruised fine, and some whole pepper. Boil it all up together, let it stand till cold, then pour it over the cabbage, and tie the jar over with leather. — AMERICAN HOME COOK-BOOK. (*By per. Dick & Fitzgerald, Pubs.*)

To Pickle Mushrooms.

Take button mushrooms; rub and clean them with flannel and salt; throw some salt over them, and lay them in a stew-pan with mace and pepper. While the liquor comes from them, keep shaking them well till the whole is dried into them again; then pour in as much vinegar as will cover them; warm them on the fire, and turn them into a jar.

Mushrooms prepared in this manner are excellent, and will keep for two years. — AMERICAN HOME COOK-BOOK. (*By per. Dick & Fitzgerald, Pubs.*)

Pickled Eggs.

Boil one or two dozen eggs until hard; when cool enough, remove the shells carefully, and then put the eggs in a jar containing vinegar in which beets have been pickled. They will become a deep red, or fine pink, according to the hue of the beets. In serving the eggs, cut off a thin slice from the large end, which will make them stand upright on the dish, and stick several cloves in the top of each. They look very pretty, and are as good as they look.

To Pickle Nasturtiums.

Take green nasturtiums fresh from the vines; put them in salt and water for one day, then drain in a napkin. Put them in glass jars, and cover with strong vinegar; keep the bottles closely corked. Are equal to capers, with roast lamb. — PRESBYTERIAN COOK-BOOK. *Dayton, O.* (*By per.*)

Pickled Barberries.

Soak nice large bunches of barberries in salt and water for a few hours. Remove from the water, and pour scalding vinegar over them. Spice the vinegar if you prefer. These are ornamental for salad-garnishing. They may be kept for some time in the brine, and freshened when used. — THE PEERLESS COOK-BOOK: *Mrs. D. A. Lincoln. Redding & Co., Pubs.* (*By per.*)

To Pickle Walnuts.

Take one hundred walnuts soft enough to allow a needle to pass through them; lay them in water, with a good handful of salt, for two days, then change to fresh water and another handful of salt for three days; then drain, and lay them on some clean straw or a sieve, in the sun, until quite black and wrinkled; afterwards put into a clean, dry glass bottle or jar a quarter of an ounce of allspice, quarter of an ounce of mace, quarter of an ounce of ginger, half a pint of mustard-seed, and half an ounce of peppercorns; these to be mixed in layers with the walnuts until your walnuts are all used; then pour over them boiling vinegar to cover them. Ready for use in two months. — *Godey's Lady's Book.* (*By per.*)

Tomato Catsup. No. 1.

Take a half-bushel tomatoes, and peel, steam, and strain them; then boil down, and add one tablespoonful ginger, one-half tablespoonful of cloves, two of cinnamon, one of mace, one teaspoonful mustard, one-half teaspoonful red pepper, two-thirds teacup of salt, and one pint of cider-vinegar. — *Osborn (O.) Local.*

Tomato Catsup. No. 2.

"Take ripe tomatoes, and scald them just sufficient to allow you to take off the skin; then let them stand for a day covered with salt; strain them thoroughly to remove the seeds; then to every two quarts add three ounces of cloves, two of black pepper, two nutmegs, and a very little cayenne-pepper, with a little salt. Boil the liquor for half an hour, then let it cool and settle; add a pint of the best cider-vinegar, after which bottle it, corking and sealing it tightly. Keep it always in a cool place."

Cucumber Catsup.

Take one peck of large, ripe cucumbers, peel, slice in half, and take out the seeds; chop very fine; add one dozen onions, also chopped fine; salt them well, and put to drain in a thin muslin bag for twenty-four hours. When taken out, season with one tablespoonful each of black and white mustard-seed, and one large teaspoonful of black pepper; mix thoroughly, and add vinegar enough to cover well. (A little grated horseradish is an improvement.) Put in glass jars or bottles. — *Lizzie Strohm.*

Grape Catsup.

Five pints grapes, three pounds sugar, one pint of vinegar, cloves and cinnamon unground. Take the skins from the pulp, and cook the latter until you can separate it from the seeds; then boil the sugar, vinegar, pulp, and spices fifteen or twenty minutes, and just before taking off add the skins. — *Osborn (O.) Local.*

Spiced Currants.

"Five pounds of currants, four pounds sugar, one pint of vinegar, four teaspoonfuls of cinnamon, four of cloves. Boil three hours. No pepper or salt. Delightful with venison or mutton."

Pear Pickles.

Take half a peck of pears halved and cored, lay the pieces together, and pack them all closely in a preserving-kettle. Add two ounces of cinnamon-bark and half an ounce of cloves, two pounds of sugar, and one pint of vinegar; cover them up, and set on a slow fire to boil. Boil down until thoroughly cooked, requiring two or three hours. Put in a stone jar, and cover with white paper wet with brandy. — *Mrs. Matilda J. Anderson, Dayton, O.*

Pickled Muskmelon.

Take a ripe melon (cantaloupe), peel, and cut in blocks. Then take two tablespoonfuls of pulverized alum dissolved in hot water, pour over, and add cold water until they are covered. (Press them down with a plate.) Let them stand over night, then drain off, and *rinse well* in cold water. Take a quart of vinegar and two pounds of sugar, boil, and pour over. Do this for nine mornings, adding to the vinegar and sugar if necessary. The ninth morning tie up in a thin muslin bag an ounce of cloves and two ounces of cinnamon-bark, boil in the vinegar, then add your melon, and boil a short time. In putting the pickle away in a jar, place the muslin bag containing the spices, among them on the top : it aids in preserving the flavor. — *Mrs. Matilda J. Anderson.*

CHAPTER XI.

PRESERVES, JAMS, AND JELLIES.

PRESERVES, JAMS, AND JELLIES.

To Preserve Peaches.

"The clear-stone yellow peaches, white at the stone, are the best. Weigh the fruit after it is pared. To each pound of fruit allow a pound of sugar. Put a layer of sugar at the bottom of the preserving-kettle, and then a layer of fruit, and so on until the fruit is all in. Stand it over the fire until the sugar is entirely dissolved; then boil them until they are clear; take them out piece by piece, and spread them on a dish free from sirup. Boil the sirup in the pan until it jellies; when the peaches are cold, fill the jars half full with them, and fill up with boiling sirup. Let them stand a short time covered with a thin cloth; then put on brandied paper, and cover them close with corks, skin, or paper. From twenty to thirty minutes will generally be sufficient to preserve them."

Peach Leather.

Stew as many peaches as you choose, allowing a quarter of a pound of sugar to one of fruit; mash it up smooth as it cooks; when it is dry enough to spread in a thin sheet on a board greased with butter, set it out in the sun to dry; and when dry it can be rolled up like leather, wrapped up in a cloth, and will keep perfectly from season to season. School children regard it as a delightful addition to their lunch of biscuit or cold bread. Apple and quince leather are made in the same fashion, only a little flavoring of spice or lemon is added to them. These leathers are made in the Valley of Virginia, and seldom seen elsewhere in the State. — VIRGINIA COOKERY-BOOK: *Mary Stuart Smith. Harper & Brothers, Pubs.* (*By per.*)

To Preserve Pears.

For preserving, small pears are better than large ones. Pare them, and make a sirup with their weight of sugar and a little water. Leave the stem on, and stick a clove in the blossom end of each. Stew till perfectly transparent. — *Arthur's Home Magazine.* (*By per.*)

Preserved Cherries.

Stone, and to every pound take a pound of sugar. Place the fruit and sugar in your kettle in alternate layers, and boil and skim until the cherries are tender and the sirup is rich. — *Arthur's Home Magazine.* (*By per.*)

Preserved Crab Apple.

"Take the red Siberian crab-apple; leave the stems on, and heat slowly to boiling in water sufficient to cover them. When the skins break, skim them out of the pan, and remove the skins. Allow one and one-fourth pounds of sugar and one teacup of water to every pound of fruit. Boil water and sugar until the scum ceases to rise. To the sirup add the juice of one lemon to every three pounds of fruit; add the fruit, boil until tender, and can immediately."

To Preserve Watermelon-Rinds.

Do not cut your rinds too thin; pare off the outside green rind; soak them two days in clean soft water, and then drain them. Take six pounds of sugar and three pints of water, boil to a thick sirup; then add your watermelon-rinds, and boil until they are clear; flavor with orange-flower water; cool, and put away in jars for use. — *Godey's Lady's Book.* (*By per.*)

Tomato Preserves.

"Take the round yellow variety as soon as ripe; scald and peel; then to seven pounds of tomatoes add seven pounds of white sugar, and let them stand over night; take the tomatoes out of the sugar, and boil the sirup, removing the scum; put in the tomatoes, and boil gently fifteen or twenty minutes; remove the fruit again, and boil until the sirup thickens. On cooling, put the fruit into jars, and pour the sirup over it, and add a few slices of lemon to each jar, and you will have something to please the taste of the most fastidious."

To Preserve Tomatoes.

In many gardens there is a plentiful supply of green tomatoes yet on the vines, that will not ripen. Allow one-half pound of white sugar to one pound of fruit. Put into the preserving-pan, and add just enough water to make sufficient sirup. Do not put too much water at first, as you can add it if there is not enough. Lemons should be sliced and put into it in the proportion of one lemon to every two pounds of fruit. Cook until done through, and the sirup looks thick. They make an excellent preserve, and taste much like preserved figs. — *Public Ledger, Philadelphia.* (*By per.*)

Preserved Barberries.

Stem the barberries, then drop them either into molasses that has been boiling ten minutes (at the rate of a quart of fruit to a pint of molasses) or in half molasses and half sugar, and then boil ten to fifteen minutes, and skim out, and boil sirup slowly about ten or fifteen minutes longer; then take off, and drop berries in. The addition of hard sweet apples is considered an improvement. Pare and quarter these, drop them in after berries are skimmed out, and boil ten or fifteen minutes, or until apples are cooked; when take off, and put back the berries. — *J. J. H. Gregory.* (*By per.*)

Quince Cheese.

"Have fine ripe quinces, and pare and core them. Cut them into pieces, and weigh them, and to each pound of the cut quinces allow half a pound of the best brown sugar. Put the cores and parings into a kettle with water enough to cover them, keeping the lid of the kettle closed. When you find that they are all boiled to pieces, and quite soft, strain off the water over the sugar, and when it is entirely dissolved, put it over the fire, and boil to a thick sirup, skimming it well. When no more scum rises, put in the quinces, cover them closely, and boil them all day over a slow fire, stirring them and mashing them down with a spoon till they are a thick, smooth paste. Then take it out, and put it into buttered tin pans or deep dishes. Let it set to get cold. It will turn out so firm that you may cut it into slices, like cheese. Keep it in a dry place, in broad stone pots. It is intended for the tea-table."

Apple Butter.

Boil a barrel of new cider down one half; then dip it out into jars, and put in the kettle a couple of buckets of cider not boiled. In this put three bushels of apples nicely pared and cut in quarters. When stewed to a sauce, add the boiled cider. (Keep adding this until all is used.) Stir constantly eight or ten hours. When done, spice with a teacupful of cinnamon, and half as much of cloves. Put away in jars; when cool, cover nicely with paper.

Strawberry Jam.

Put the fruit into a jar, and stand this in a pan of boiling water over the fire. As the boiling proceeds, keep mashing the strawberries with a wooden spatula until they are all bruised to a pulp. Then put them into a preserving-pan, and to every pound add three-quarters of a pound of sugar. Boil the whole until of due consistence, which will occupy more than half an hour, keeping the jam in constant agitation lest the bottom should burn. When done enough, take it off the fire, and put it into pots. —*Peterson's Magazine.* (*By per.*)

Raspberry Jam.

Let the raspberries be thoroughly ripe. Mash them with a wooden spoon. To every pound of raspberries add a pound of sifted sugar. Boil this well together during half an hour, stirring it continually lest it should burn. When of a good thickness, put it into pots, and proceed to tie up. —*Peterson's Magazine.* (*By per.*)

Blackberry Jam.

Six quarts of ripe berries and three pounds of brown sugar. Mash together, and put into a kettle and boil two hours, stirring frequently. Spice to taste, or omit spices altogether. When cool, put it into a jar, cover with brandied paper, and seal, and it will keep for years. —*Arthur's Home Magazine.* (*By per.*)

Gooseberry Jam.

"Stew the berries in a little water, put them through a coarse sieve, put them back into the kettle, add three-quarters of a pound of sugar to each pound of the stewed berries. Boil for about three-quarters of an hour; and they will need constant stirring, or they will certainly burn. You can easily determine whether a jam requires more boiling, by taking a small quantity out on a saucer. If it looks bright and glistening, and no water-like juice surrounds it on the saucer, it is safe to infer that it is done."

Rhubarb Jam. No. 1.

"To seven pounds of rhubarb add four sweet oranges and five pounds of sugar. Peel and cut up the rhubarb. Put in the thin peel of the oranges and the pulp, after taking out the seeds and all the whites. Boil all together for an hour and a half."

Rhubarb Jam. No. 2.

"It is best made in June, when the rhubarb is no longer young. Take ten pounds of large-sized rhubarb, and cut it up; add to it one pound of candied peel (viz., citron, lemon, and orange) shred, and also the rind of two large fresh lemons chopped fine, one pound of sugar to the same weight of fruit, and boil like other preserve."

Crab-Apple Jam.

Pare the crab-apples when quite ripe. Put them into a stone jar, cover it well, and put it in a pan of boiling water for an hour and a half. Then prepare the sirup with two pounds of sugar in half a pint of water, for every pound of the apples. Clarify the sirup. Then put the apples into it, and boil the whole to a jam. — *Peterson's Magazine.* (*By per.*)

Pine-apple Marmalade.

To every pound of grated pine-apple allow a pound of double-refined loaf-sugar. Boil until thick; then pack in tumblers, and paste over them papers wet with the beaten whites of eggs. Keep them in a dry cool place until wanted. — *Godey's Lady's Book.* (*By per.*)

Apple Jelly.

Cut off all spots and decayed places on the apples; quarter them, but do not pare or core them; put in the peel of as many lemons as you like, about two to six or eight dozen of the apples; fill the preserving-pan, and cover the fruit with spring-water; boil them till they are in pulp, then pour them into a jelly-bag; let them strain all night, do not squeeze them. To every pint of juice put one pound of white sugar; put in the juice of the lemons you had before pared, but strain it through muslin; you may also put in about a teaspoonful of essence of lemon. Let it boil for at least twenty minutes; it will look redder than at first; skim it well all the time. Put it either in shapes or pots, and cover it the next day. It ought to be quite stiff and very clear. — *Godey's Lady's Book.* (*By per. Pub.*)

Cider Apple Jelly.

"Cut good, ripe apples in quarters, put them in a kettle, and cover them with *sweet* cider just from the press. (It should, if possible, be used the day it is made, or, at any rate, before it has worked at all.) Boil until well done, and drain through a sieve. Do not press it through. Measure the liquor, and to each pint add one pound of sugar. Boil from twenty minutes to half an hour."

Quince and Apple Jelly.

"Cut small, and core, an equal weight of tart apples and quinces; put the quinces in a preserving-kettle, with water to cover them, and boil till soft; add the apples, still keeping water to cover them, and boil till the whole is nearly a pulp; put the whole into a jelly-bag, and strain without pressing. To each quart of juice allow two pounds of lump-sugar. Boil together half an hour."

Currant Jelly.

Pick fine red but long-ripe currants from the stems; bruise them, and strain the juice from a quart at a time through a thin muslin; wring it gently, to get all the liquid; put a pound of white sugar to each pint of juice; stir it until it is all dissolved; set it over a gentle fire, let it become hot, and boil for fifteen minutes. Then try it by taking a spoonful into a saucer; when cold, if it is not quite firm enough, boil it for a few minutes longer. — *Godey's Lady's Book.* (*By per.*)

Elderberry Jelly.

Heat the berries, and press out the juice, and to every pint of it add a half-pint of sugar. Boil until it becomes a *thick* sirup. The elderberries alone will not make a jelly firm enough to turn out of tumblers or bowls, but if the juice of *grapes* is added to it, — about one-third of a pint to a pint of elderberries, — it then becomes very firm and solid. — *Miss Lizzie Strohm.*

Grape Jelly.

"Strip from their stalks some fine ripe black-cluster grapes, and stir them with a wooden spoon over a gentle fire until all have burst, and the juice flows freely from them; strain it off without pressure, and pass it through a jelly-bag, or through a twice-folded muslin; weigh, and then boil it rapidly for twenty minutes; draw it from the fire, stir in it till dissolved fourteen ounces of good sugar, roughly powdered, to each pound of juice, and boil the jelly quickly for fifteen minutes longer, keeping it constantly stirred, and perfectly well skimmed. It will be perfectly clear, and of a beautiful pale rose-color."

Red-Haw Jelly.

Wash the haws well, and put on in a kettle with water sufficient to almost cover them (not too much water). Boil until they are soft. When cool enough, express the juice thoroughly through a thin muslin cloth. To three pints of juice add two pints of granulated sugar, and boil until it bubbles. Less boiling will answer if it is not desired to mould into "shapes" or "designs." It is a firm and handsome jelly for moulds. The taste is delicious, resembling *guava* jelly. — *Lizzie Strohm.*

Strawberry Jelly.

The fruit, in the first place, should be as fresh from the vines as is possible to obtain it, and free from all sand or dirt. After picking the hulls from them, put the berries into an enamelled preserving-pan, and set it by the side of the fire to draw out the juice. As soon as this begins to flow freely, place the pan over a slow fire, and allow the berries to simmer very gently until they begin to soften, being careful to remove it before the juice commences to thicken. Then pour them upon a clean, dry sieve, and when the juice has drained thoroughly through, strain it through two or three thicknesses of muslin, and, after weighing it, put it again into the preserving-pan. Let it boil briskly for twenty minutes, stirring frequently, then remove it from the fire, and add the sugar, allowing fourteen ounces to each pound of the juice. (Loaf-sugar broken in small lumps is the best for the purpose, and should be added a little at a time.) As soon as the sugar becomes dissolved, place the pan again on the fire, and let the jelly boil until done. To test this, take a little out, and put it on a plate or saucer; if it stiffens, it is done enough. Then pour it into jars, cover tightly, and set in a cool dry place till wanted for use. — *The Caterer.* (*By per.*)

CHAPTER XII.

BREAD, RUSK, BUNS, ROLLS, AND BISCUIT.

BREAD, RUSK, BUNS, ROLLS, AND BISCUIT.

AUNT CINDY'S DINNER.

"WELL, Cindy," said the Rev. Mr. Burgiss, "you air goin' to have a chance to-morrow to distinguish you'self."

Cindy was a tall and fleshy woman, weighing three hundred and seventeen pounds. She was sitting on the block which was seat or meat-slab, as the occasion demanded. She rose from this block with a heaving, labored motion, which called to mind a steamboat getting under way. "I's tolerbul distinguished a'ready," she replied. Perhaps the speaker found a difficulty in raising and lowering her astonishing lower jaw and double chin. Her words had a queer, smothered sound, as though coming through hot mush. "What's gwyne on ter-morrer?" she asked.

"Why, we air goin' to have fou' persidin' elduz yere to dinner to-morrow, — yes, fou' presidin' elduz."

"Good gracious!" exclaimed Aunt Cindy, almost overwhelmed. "Mussy on us! fou' puzzidin' elduz! Reckons I hab ter stir my stumps tolerbul lively 'bout dat dar dinner;" and her eyes, hid away in rolls of fat, like pin-heads in a cushion, began to twinkle in anticipation of a culinary triumph. "But," she continued, clouding again, "we-all ain't got no little pig. Can't git no dinner fit for shucks widouten a pig roas' whole, wid a red apple in its mouf. Mus' hab a pig somehows, to be sartin."

"Oh, we can get a pig," said Mr. Burgiss assuredly. "Jus' sen' Tony over to Brother Phillpotts's early in the mawnin' to bórrer one. Tell him to tell Sister Phillpotts that I'll return it the fus' chance. An' now, Cindy, my girl, jus' do you' bes' on that dinner."

"'Deed, I'll do my very bes'. Puffidin' dinner for fou' puzzidin' elduz is a heap er 'spons'bil'ty, but I reckons yer'll fin' ole Cindy kin tote it. Jes' don't worrit you'se'f." . . .

"Dat light-bread ought to be sot ter raisin'," Aunt Cindy soliloquized when left alone. She spread out a fat hand on each knee, and helped herself up from the meat-block. Then she mounted the bench that served as her observatory, and began searching the log sleeper, rummaging among the various paper parcels. "Wonder what's gone wid dem twin brudders," she said (Aunt Cindy was looking for a small package of Twin Brothers yeast cakes, which some Yankee had introduced in the neighborhood). "Dat dar Tony's gone an' toted off dem dar twin brudders, I'll be boun'. — To-nee! To-nee!" she called, at the height of her muffled voice. "I see yer sneakin' 'hin' dat dar chicken-coop. Yere'd better come yere, 'fo' I comes dar an' fotches yer wid a peach-tree limb. Hurry 'long outen dat dar snail's pace."

Tony appeared, looking like a tattered scarecrow with a live head.

"Whar's dem dar twin brudders? I wants ter put one uv um ter soak. What yer gone an' done wid dem dar twin brudders?" persisted Aunt Cindy.

"I hain't done nuffin 't all wid dem dar twin brudders,—nebber tetched um," Tony declared, half frightened, half sullen.

"Hush you' mouf, yer story-teller! I'll be boun' yer's gone an' feeded all dem twin brudders to de chickens. Yer's too lazy ter mix a little cawn-meal fer um."

"Nebber feeded dem dar twin brudders to de chickens, no more'n nuffin," Tony insisted.

"How yer reckons I'se gwine ter git dinner fer dem fou' puzzidin' elduz ef I hain't got no twin brudders to make de light-bread?"

"I dun know."

"Ob cou'se yer dun know; yer dun know nuffin. Come yere while I boxes you' jaw. I boxes yer kase I lubbed you' gran'mudder. Me an' her uster play togedder when we all wus bofe gals togedder."

Aunt Cindy was heaving and balancing herself, preparatory to a descent from the bench on which she was mounted. Down she stepped at length, her broad bare foot meeting the dirt floor with a heavy thud,—or slap, rather.

"Come 'long up yere," continued Aunt Cindy. Tony was moving towards her with a reluctant, bewildered air, his dead grandmother and the twin brothers all in a jumble in his brain, when Aunt Cindy suddenly exclaimed, "Dar's dem twin brudders now, on dat dar jam!" Tony smiled from ear to ear, in his satisfaction at having escaped the impending boxing. "Hush you' grinnin' dar, yer imperance, an' go 'long an' fotch me some hick'ry-bo'k to cook dat dinner. Wasn't yer 'ware I's got ter git dinner fer fou' puzzidin' elduz?"

Tony gave a long whistle of astonishment, and went off toward the woods.

While the yeast-cake was soaking, Aunt Cindy set to work collecting materials for a cake; a pound-cake with icing, she had decided upon. Although her movements were slow and labored, there were strength and force in them, so that she accomplished a surprising amount of work. She didn't lose much time looking for spoons and forks. She stirred things with her finger, and with it she tested her gravies and sauces and custards. It needed but a few strokes of her warm, strong hand, to beat the butter to a cream: a few turns more, and the sugar was thoroughly incorporated with this. Then with some twigs of crape-myrtle, in lieu of an egg-beater, the yolk of the eggs was soon foaming, and the white standing alone. Lastly, she bethought her of the cinnamon to make it "tasty," she said. Panting and blowing, she again ascended her observatory, and began snuffing, tasting, and peering at the various paper parcels on the log sleeper. "Whar kin dat cin'mon-bok be at?" she said. "I hain't seed it sence I tuk it to meetin' to scent my han'kercher. I'll be bound dat dar Tony's done gone an' tuck an' et dat dar cin'mon-bok, ha'r an' hide. Maybe I put it in de big gou'd."

She waddled down from the bench and across the shed to a gourd as large as a giant pumpkin, and with much the shape of one. She turned it bottom up on the dirt floor, and out poured an incredible assortment of things: a fork, three partridge-eggs, a head-kerchief, a pair of slippers, a dish-towel, two peaches, a purple belt-ribbon, a phial of hair-oil, a hymn-book, a lump of loaf-sugar, a stick of sassafras-root, a paper of saleratus, and another of snuff. "'Tain't yere." She looked the jambs over, and then, with a majestic waddle, she crossed the yard to the house.

"Miss Rithy," she said, when she found herself in Mrs. Burgiss's presence, "I ain't gwine ter take de 'spons'bil'ty uv no poun'-cake widouten cin'mon-bok to puffume it, an' I hain't got no cin'mon-bok on my premsis."

"Sen' over to Brother Phillpotts's an' borrer a stick," said the lady appealed to, returning to her perforated cardboard, on which she was working in rainbow worsteds a church with a man beside it. The man was taller than the steeple. . . .

In process of time, Tony appeared with three small pieces of bark, and was, properly or improperly, belabored by Aunt Cindy's tongue, she declaring that she could "eat all dat dar bok," and demanding to be told how she was "gwine ter cook dinner fer fou' puzzidin' elduz wid dat thimbulful of bok? An' my cakes a-sottin' yere waitin' all dis while, an' all dat 'nifikent white froff gittin' limber, an' all de lather done gone outen dat dar yaller! An' I beat dat dar egg tell my arm ache to de morrer-bone. Yer go 'long an' hurry an' cotch ole Jack, an' go to Mis' Phillpotts's ter borrer somethin'."

Tony hurried off, glad to get away from Aunt Cindy and her uncertain moods. It was over an hour, however, before he got started for Mrs. Philpotts's; for first he had to indulge himself in repeated climbings and slidings on the fodder-stacks; then in divers tumblings and leapings in the straw-pen; then he "skinned the cat" a few dozen times; then he had a thrilling ride round and round the barnyard, swinging on old Jack's tail; then he made a raid on some blackberry-bushes in the fence-corner, where he ate berries as long and thick as his thumb for ten minutes. Then he put a bridle on the old gray mule, mounted its bare back, and entered upon a course of pullings, tuggings, and kickings, to the end of making the said mule go forward to Mrs. Phillpotts's, instead of backward to its stall, as it seemed determined to do. As all the boy's thoughts and energies were thus engaged, it never occurred to him that he didn't know what he was going for, until he stood in Mrs. Phillpotts's presence, feeling and looking very foolish. Nothing remained to be done but to remount his gallant steed, return to Aunt Cindy, and ascertain the nature of the something he was to borrow from Mrs. Phillpotts. Oh, how he shrunk from the forthcoming interview with Aunt Cindy! Her dreaded hands doubled in size to his frightened fancy, and his ears seemed to tingle with the inevitable boxing which Aunt Cindy would be certain to feel it her duty to administer, because she loved his grandmother.

"Wish she nebber lubbed my gran'mammy — wish she hate my gran'mammy," Tony whispered to his beating heart, as on went old Jack at a spanking, bouncing trot, that threatened to unhorse the rider. It seemed to Tony that no other mule ever trotted so relentlessly. He clung desperately to the bridle and the roached mane, and was trotted on by the merciless brute past the house, through the barnyard, and into the stable, Tony throwing himself almost under the belly to save himself from being rubbed off in the low doorway.

"Whyn't yer spen' de night at Mis' Phillpotts's?" Cindy asked, when he appeared in her presence, his eyes distended and rolling in frightened anticipation. "Dat white's done gone back twict, waitin' on you' lazy bones. Nobody but a bawn cook could fotch a poun'-cake fit fer fou' puzzidin' elduz outen sich trib'lations. Don't yer know I's got ter git dinner fer fou' puzzidin' elduz? But, law! yer wouldn't kere ef dey wus fou' bishops. What do yer kere 'bout rerligion? Yer's so wicked! Gim me that cin'mon-bok, and don't stan' dar shilly-shally, like a gobbler on hot tin."

Then came Tony's acknowledgment that he had gone all the way to Mrs. Phillpotts's without once thinking that he did not know what he was going for. You should have seen how Aunt Cindy received this, when the idea had fairly taken possession of her mind. It went to her funny spot. Planting her hands, outspread, on her sides, as if to fortify herself against shaking to pieces, she began laughing almost without a sound, as though she was too well cushioned to make any noise. She quivered all over like a great mass of jelly, swaying back and forth, her head falling on her chest, on this shoulder and on that, till she fell with a great flop on the meat-block, where she continued to sway and roll and quiver. Tony's intense appreciation of the turned tide, expressed in broad grins, in titters, in giggles, in shuffles, in balancings, in hand-rubbings, was about as funny as Aunt Cindy's characteristic laughing. Before this laughing was ended, he had made good his escape, and in process of events was repeating his tuggings and pullings at old Jack's bridle. It was dark before he returned from his errand; for Mrs. Phillpotts not having any cinnamon, had sent a runner to Mrs. McDonald for the article. Mrs. McDonald, in turn, had sent to Mrs. Doubleday, and Mrs. Doubleday to the cross-roads store. Aunt Cindy never went to bed that night — never went to her cabin: she sat up with her cake and light-bread. — AUNT CINDY'S DINNER: *Sarah Winter Kellogg. From Lippincott's Magazine.* (*By per.*)

Yeast.

Ingredients: One teacupful of lightly broken hops, or, if the Shaker packages are used, half a teacupful; one pint of sifted flour; one teacupful of granulated sugar; one tablespoonful of salt; four large or six medium-sized potatoes; two quarts boiling water. Boil the potatoes; drain off the water when done, and let them dry off a few minutes, precisely as for table. At the same time, having tied the hops in a cloth, boil them half an hour in the two quarts of water, renewing it if it boils away. Mix the flour, sugar, and salt well together in a large mixing-bowl, and pour on the boiling hop-water slowly, stirring constantly. Now add enough of this to the mashed potato to thin it till it can be poured, and mix it all together, straining it through a sieve to avoid any possible lumps. Add to this, when cool, either a cupful of yeast left from the last, or of baker's yeast, or a cake of compressed yeast dissolved in a little warm water. Let it stand two hours or so till partly light, then stir it down two or three times in the course of five or six hours, as this makes it stronger. At the end of that time it will be light. Keep in a carefully corked stone jug, or in glass cans, the last being the best; and in all cases be particular to have whatever holds it perfectly sweet and well scalded. Be as careful with stopper or cover as with the vessel itself.

For dry yeast, stir in corn-meal till a dough is made, form it in small, thin cakes, and dry them carefully in the sun. For hot weather this is a convenient form, as it does not sour. Crumb and soak in warm water half an hour before using.

Potato yeast is made by omitting hops and flour, but mashing the potatoes fine with the other ingredients, and adding the old yeast when cool, as before. The number of potatoes can be doubled, or left the same. It is very nice, but must be made fresh every week; while the other, kept in a cool place, will be good a month. — *Mrs. Helen Campbell. From Good Housekeeping. (By per. Pubs.)*

Bread.

For four medium-sized loaves of bread allow as follows: Four quarts of flour; one large cup of yeast (half a pint); one tablespoonful of salt, one of sugar, and one of butter or lard; one pint of milk mixed with one of warm water, or one quart of water alone, for the "wetting." Sift the flour into a large pan or bowl. Put the sugar, salt, and shortening, in the bottom of the bread-pan or bowl, and pour on a spoonful or two of boiling water, enough to dissolve all; add the quart of wetting and the yeast. . Now stir in, slowly, two quarts of the flour, beating well; cover with a thick cloth, and set in a temperature of about seventy-five degrees to rise until morning. Bread mixed at nine in the evening will be ready to mould into loaves or rolls by six the next morning. In summer it would be necessary to find a cool place; in winter, a warm one; the chief point being to keep the temperature *even*. If mixed early in the morning, it is ready to mould and bake in the afternoon, from seven to eight hours being all that it should stand. This first mixture is called a *sponge;* and if only a single loaf of Graham or rye bread is wanted, one quart of it can be measured and thickened with either flour as in the rules given hereafter. To finish as *wheat bread*, stir in flour from the two quarts remaining to make a dough. Flour the moulding-board very thickly, and turn out. Now begin kneading, flouring the hands, but after the dough is gathered in a smooth lump, using as little flour as may be; knead with the palm of the hand as much as possible. The dough quickly becomes a flat cake. Fold it over, and keep on kneading, not less than twenty minutes, half an hour being better. Make into loaves; put into the pans; set them in a warm place, and let them rise from thirty to forty-five minutes, or until they have become nearly double in size. Bake in an oven hot enough to brown a teaspoonful of flour in five minutes, spreading the flour on a bit of broken plate that it may have an even heat. The pan is an important point, the best being made of block-tin or Russia iron. A brick loaf bakes most easily, and it is quite worth while to have a set of bread-pans made to order, ten inches long by four wide and four deep. Loaves of this size will bake in from forty-five to sixty minutes. Then take them from the pans, wrap them in thick cloths kept for the purpose, and stand them tilted up against the pans till cold. Never lay hot bread on a pine table, as it will sweat, and absorb the pitchy odor and taste; but tilt so that the air will pass around it freely. Keep well covered in a tin box or large stone pot, which should be wiped out every day or two, and scalded and dried thoroughly in the sun once a week. Pans for wheat bread should be greased very lightly; for Graham or rye, much more, as the dough sticks and clings. Instead of mixing a sponge, all the flour may be moulded in and kneaded at once, and the dough set to rise in the same way; when light, turn out. Use as little flour as possible, and knead fifteen minutes; less time being required, as part of the kneading has already been done. — *Mrs. Helen Campbell. From Good Housekeeping.* (*By per. Pubs.*)

To Test the Oven.

Throw on the floor of the oven a tablespoonful of new flour; if it takes fire, or assumes a dark-brown color, the temperature is too high, and the oven must be allowed to cool. If the flour remains white after the lapse of a few seconds, the temperature is too low. When the oven is of the proper temperature, the flour will turn a brownish yellow, and look slightly scorched. — BREAKFAST DAINTIES: *Thomas J. Murrey. White, Stokes, & Allen, Pubs.*

Vienna Bread.

"Two pounds sifted flour banked around pan, one-half pint milk, one-half pint water; mix a thin batter; quickly add one-half pint milk, in which has been dissolved one-half ounce salt and seven-eighths ounce compressed yeast; leave remainder of flour against side of pan; cover and keep free from air forty-five minutes; then mix in rest of the flour until dough leaves side and bottom of pan. Let stand for two and a half hours. Divide into one-pound pieces. Subdivide into twelve pieces. Fold corner of each piece to centre, turn over to rise for thirty minutes. Put in hot oven, bake twenty minutes."

French Twist Bread.

Take one quart of light dough raised with home-made yeast; mix in a large tablespoonful of sweet butter, a saltspoon of salt, and one egg; add flour, and knead well. Let it rise until light, then knead very gently; roll the dough in thin strips, measuring an inch in diameter; dredge lightly with flour, and braid loosely; let it stand a few moments, and bake quickly without burning. — *Peterson's Magazine.* (*By per.*)

Aërated Home-made Bread.

Mix flour and water together to the consistency of a thick batter; then beat it until fine bubbles of air thoroughly permeate it; for small biscuit, pour it into patty-pans, and bake in a good brisk oven; for bread in loaves, more flour is thoroughly kneaded in with the hands, until the dough is full of air-bubbles, and then baked at once, without being allowed to stand. — COOKING MANUAL: *Juliet Corson. Dodd, Mead, & Co., Pubs.* (*By per.*)

Gems.

These are the simplest form of bread, and if properly made are certain to be light and sweet. A hot oven and hot pans are prime essentials, and there must be no delay between making and baking. The coldest water, ice-water preferred, should be used. Use either whole-wheat flour or Graham, three parts of flour to one of water being the right proportion. For a dozen gems allow one large cup — a half-pint — of ice-water, one even teaspoonful of salt, and three cups of flour. Stir in the flour slowly, beating hard and steadily, not less than ten minutes. The pans should have been set on top of the stove, and oiled or buttered. Fill them two-thirds full, and bake about half an hour. If properly made, they are very light, and have the full flavor of the wheat. Hygienic cook-books give the same rule as practicable for bread, but none tested by the writer has ever been really eatable. Gems can be freshened by dipping in cold water and heating quickly, but it is best to make no more than will be eaten at once. Rye can be used, but with less certainty of a good result. — *Mrs. Helen Campbell. From Good Housekeeping. (By per Pubs.)*

Salt-Rising Bread.

Put half a teaspoonful of salt in half a teacupful of flour; pour on boiling water; work it well very stiff; put this where it will keep warm all night; next morning take a pint of milk, warm water, and as much salt as before; mix in flour till you make a good muffin-batter; then add the scalded yeast to the batter, and set it in warm water till it rises; then add flour to form a stiff dough, and bake. This is the favorite bread all through the Valley of Virginia and Maryland. Some dyspeptics think it much more digestible than bread made up with other kinds of yeast. — VIRGINIA COOKERY-BOOK: *Mrs. Mary Stuart Smith. (By per. Harper & Brothers, Pubs.)*

We found Mr. *Agnew* equallie busie with his Apples, mounted ha'f way up one of the Trees, and throwing Cherry Pippins down into *Rose's* Apron, and now and then making as though he would pelt her: onlie she dared him, and woulde not be frightened. Her Donkey, chewing Apples in the Corner, with the Cider running out of his Mouth, presented a ludicrous Image of Enjoyment, and 'twas evidently enhanct by *Giles'* brushing his rough Coat with a Birch Besom, instead of minding his owne businesse of sweeping the Walk. The Sun, shining with mellow Light on the mown Grass and fresh clipt Hornbeam Hedges, made even the commonest Objects distinct and cheerfulle; and the Air was soe cleare, we coulde hear the Village Children afar off at theire Play.

Rose had abundance of delicious new Honey in the Comb, and Bread hot from the oven, for our earlie Supper. — MARY POWELL: *Mrs. Manning.*

Honey without the comb is the perfume without the rose, — it is sweet merely, and soon degenerates into candy. Half the delectableness is in breaking down these frail and exquisite walls yourself, and tasting the nectar before it has lost its freshness by contact with the air. — LOCUSTS AND WILD HONEY: *John Burroughs. Houghton, Mifflin, & Co., Pubs.* (*By per.*)

Rusk.

One cup milk scalded and cooled; one tablespoonful sugar; one-half teaspoonful salt; one-quarter cup yeast; two cups flour.

Mix in a sponge at night, or very early in the morning. When well risen, add flour enough to make a stiff dough. Knead and let it rise again, then add *one-fourth* of *a cup* of *butter* rubbed to a cream, *half a cup* of *sugar*, and *one egg* beaten with butter and sugar. Let it rise in the bowl till light. Shape into small round biscuit; put them close together in a shallow cake-pan, that they may rise very high. When ready to bake, rub the tops with sugar dissolved in milk, sprinkle with dry sugar, and bake in a moderate oven. — THE BOSTON COOK-BOOK: *Mrs. D. A. Lincoln. Roberts Bros., Pubs.* (*By per.*)

Buns.

"Into a pound and a half of well-dried flour rub four ounces of moist sugar; warm a quarter of a pint of milk about blood warm, but not hot enough to scald the yeast which you will use; make a hole in the middle of your flour, and put in a quarter of a teacupful, or thereabout, of good thick yeast, which is not too bitter, or it will taste in the buns; pour on it your warm milk, and mix with it about one-third, or nearly half, of your flour, leaving the rest of the flour unmixed round the sides of your pan. Set it in a warm place to rise for three-quarters of an hour or an hour. When it has risen well, melt a quarter of a pound of butter, and mix it with milk; let it be on the fire till about blood warm, and then mix it with the rest of the flour and sugar into your dough. When mixed, it should be rather softer than bread-dough. Put it to rise for about a quarter of an hour, and then mould them; put them on buttered iron plates, and then into a warm place to rise light; when well risen, bake them in a hot oven. If you wish to have currants or caraway-seeds in them, mix them in along with the butter; if you wish them spiced, mix equal quantities of ground ginger, allspice, coriander, and caraway; put as much as you think sufficient, when you put in the butter. When they are baked enough, brush them over with egg and water mixed together, to give them a gloss."

Saffron Buns.

"Make the dough for them the same as for plain buns. Put a little of the best saffron in a teacup, and pour over a little boiling water; let it stand on the top of the oven, to extract the flavor; and when you put in the butter, mix in as much of the saffron-water as will make the dough of a bright yellow color. Bake them as before directed. You may put in a few currants, but saffron buns are seldom spiced."

Hot Cross Buns.

"Two pounds of flour, half a pound of sugar, and a small quantity of grated nutmeg and allspice mixed together. Make a hole in the centre of the flour, and into it put two tablespoonfuls of yeast, pouring in also half a pint of warm milk. With the latter and the surrounding flour make a thin batter; cover the dish, and let it stand before the fire till the leaven begins to ferment. Now add to the whole half a pound of butter melted, and sufficient milk to make all the flour into a soft paste. Dust it over with flour, and let it rise again for half an hour. Make the dough into the shape of buns, notch out on each the form of the cross, and lay them separately in rows on buttered tin plates to rise once more for half an hour; after which, put them into a quick oven, watching them carefully lest the color should be spoiled by over-baking."

Parker-House Rolls.

One teacup home-made yeast, a little salt, one tablespoonful sugar, a piece of lard size of an egg, one pint milk, flour sufficient to mix. Put the milk on the stove to scald, with the lard in it. Prepare the flour with salt, sugar, and yeast. Then add the milk, not too hot. Knead thoroughly when mixed at night; in the morning but very slight kneading is necessary. Then roll out, and cut with large biscuit-cutter. Spread a little butter on each roll, and lap together. Let them rise very light, then bake in a quick oven. — THE EVERY-DAY COOK-BOOK: *Miss Neill.* (*By per. Belford, Clarke, & Co.*)

Brown Biscuit.

Three cups of Graham flour, one cup of white flour, one tablespoonful of lard and the same of butter; one tablespoonful of brown sugar, two teaspoonfuls of baking-powder, one teaspoonful of salt, two cups of milk. Sift brown and white flour, sugar, baking-powder, salt, into a bowl; rub or chop in the shortening; wet up with the milk into a soft dough; roll out half an inch thick, handling as little as possible, and with as few strokes of the rolling-pin; cut into round cakes, and bake quickly in a floured pan. — *Marion Harland. The Post, Washington, D.C. (By per.)*

Egg Biscuit.

Two cups of warm milk, two eggs, two heaping tablespoonfuls of butter, half a cake of compressed yeast dissolved in warm water, one quart of sifted flour, one teaspoonful of salt; mix with the butter (melted but not hot) the yeast, salt, and three cups of flour together over night, and set in a covered bowl to rise. Early in the morning add the beaten eggs and the rest of the flour, and set for a second rising of an hour or longer. When light roll into a sheet almost an inch thick, cut into round cakes, and lay in a floured baking-pan. At the end of half an hour bake in a good oven. They are delicious cold or hot. — *Marion Harland. The Post, Washington, D.C. (By per.)*

Naples Biscuit.

"Beat eight eggs; add to them one pound of flour; one pound of powdered sugar, one teaspoonful of essence of lemon. Bake in a quick oven."

Soda Biscuits.

One quart of flour, a pint of buttermilk, half a teaspoonful of soda dissolved in the milk; half a teaspoonful of salt; a piece of lard about the size of a large egg, rubbed in the flour. Mix well together, roll out about an inch thick, and cut into biscuits. Bake in a quick oven. — *Mrs. Matilda J. Anderson, Dayton, O.*

Drop Biscuit.

One quart of flour, three teaspoonfuls of baking-powder, tablespoonful of sugar, half a teacup of lard worked in the flour; add sweet milk enough to make a thick batter. Drop in little pans or muffin-rings, and bake.

Flyaways, or Soufflé Biscuits.

Rub four ounces of butter into one quart of flour sifted, add a saltspoonful of salt, and make into a paste with milk. Knead well, handling lightly, and roll out until they are as thin as paper and the size of a common saucer; stick here and there with a fork, and bake in a moderate oven until they look flaky and white.

Butter, four ounces.

Flour, one quart.

Milk, one-half pint.

Salt, one saltspoonful. — Virginia Cookery-Book: *Mrs. Mary Stuart Smith. Harper & Brothers, Pubs.* (*By per.*)

Scotch Scones.

"Sift half a spoonful of soda into a quart of flour, and mix in rich buttermilk enough to make a dough as stiff as for soda-biscuit. Roll out half an inch thick, and bake on a hot griddle in two large cakes the size of dinner-plates. Serve with dishes of Dundee marmalade."

French Toast.

"Beat four eggs very light, and stir with them a pint of milk; slice some baker's bread, dip the pieces into the egg, then lay them in a pan of hot lard, and fry brown; sprinkle a little powdered sugar and cinnamon on each piece, and serve hot. If nicely prepared, this is an excellent dish for breakfast or tea."

CHAPTER XIII.

BROWN BREAD, HOT CAKES, ETC.

BROWN BREAD, HOT CAKES, ETC.

MARGARET seated herself on the door-step to eat her supper, consisting of toasted brown bread and watered cider, served in a curiously wrought cherry bowl and spoon. The family were taking their meal in the kitchen. The sun had gone down. The whippoorwill came and sat on the butternut, and sang his evening note, always plaintive, always welcome. The night-hawk dashed and hissed through the woods and the air, on slim, quivering wings. A solitary robin chanted sweetly a long time from the hill. Myriads of insects revolved and murmured over her head. Crickets chirped in the grass and under the decaying sills of the house. She heard the voice of the waterfall at the Outlet, and the croaking of a thousand frogs in the Pond. She saw the stars come out, Lyra, the Northern Crown, the Serpent. She looked into the heavens, she opened her ears to the dim evening melodies of the universe; yet as a child. She was interrupted by the sharp voice of her mother, "Go to your roost, Peggy!"

"Yes, Molly dear," said her father, very softly, "Dick and Robin are asleep: see who will be up first, you or the silver rooster; who will open your eyes first, you or the dandelion?" — MARGARET: *Sylvester Judd*. (*By per. Roberts Brothers.*)

Brown Bread.

Make ready: one *even* cup of Indian meal; two *heaping* cups of rye meal; one teaspoonful of salt, and one of soda, mixed together with the sifted meal in a large bowl; one cupful of molasses, in a quart measure or small bowl, with spoon; a large beating spoon; palette-knife, to scrape your mixture from the bowl; a tin bread or pudding boiler, well buttered.

Stir the meal, salt, and soda, dry, until thoroughly mingled. Pour one pint of hot water to the molasses, and stir it up. Pour the molasses and water into the middle of your meal, stirring to a smooth batter as in previous directions; beat all quickly and well for several minutes; it should be of a consistence to stir easily, and break in pouring, but not to run. With some qualities of molasses, you may need to add from a spoonful or two to half a cup more of warm water, to make it right.

Put into your tin boiler, cover tight, and put this into an iron kettle with boiling water in it. Cover the kettle also. Boil steadily for three hours, looking from time to time to see if the water in the kettle is boiling away. Keep it replenished, always from boiling water. Take the bread-boiler out at the end of the three hours, and set it into the oven for about ten minutes; longer if the oven is not quick. This is to dry the outside steam off, and form a tender crust. Put hot upon the table; cut and help hot. — JUST HOW: A KEY TO THE COOK-BOOKS: *Mrs. A. D. T. Whitney. Houghton, Mifflin, & Co., Pubs. (By per.)*

Maize Muffins.

Shredded maize deserves special mention, as being the highest and most scientific product of corn that has been introduced for public consideration. From it a most excellent porridge can be made in ten minutes. Griddle-cakes, sweet puddings, and especially breakfast-rolls made of it, are delightful. Most excellent muffins are prepared as follows: Mix together one pound of shredded maize, one pint of hot milk, a teaspoonful of salt, and one ounce of butter; let it cool, and whisk into it three beaten eggs, one ounce of sugar, and two teaspoonfuls of wheat baking-powder; mix thoroughly; half fill the muffin-rings, and bake in a hot oven. — BREAKFAST DAINTIES: *Thomas J. Murrey. White, Stokes, & Allen, Pubs.*

Johnny-Cake.

Sift one quart of Indian meal into a pan; make a hole in the middle, and pour in a pint of warm water, adding one teaspoonful of salt; with a spoon mix the meal and water gradually into a soft dough; stir it very briskly for a quarter of an hour or more, till it becomes light and spongy; then spread the dough smooth and evenly on a straight, flat board (a piece of the head of a flour-barrel will serve for this purpose); place the board nearly upright before an open fire, and put an iron against the back to support it; bake it well; when done, cut it in squares; send it hot to table, split and buttered. — VIRGINIA COOKERY-BOOK: *Mary Stuart Smith. Harper & Brothers, Pubs.* (*By per.*)

It was Lois and her father, — Joe Yare being feeder that night. They were in one of the great furnace-rooms in the cellar, — a very comfortable place that stormy night. Two or three doors of the wide brick ovens were open, and the fire threw a ruddy glow over the stone floor, and shimmered into the dark recesses of the shadows, very homelike after the rain and mud without. Lois seemed to think so, at any rate, for she had made a table of a store-box, put a white cloth on it, and was busy getting up a regular supper for her father, — down on her knees before the red coals, turning something on an iron plate, while some slices of ham sent up a cloud of juicy, hungry smell.

The old Stoker had just finished slaking the out-fires, and was putting some blue plates on the table, gravely straightening them. He had grown old, as Polston said, — Holmes saw, stooped much, with a low, hacking cough; his coarse clothes were curiously clean: that was to please Lois, of course. She put the ham on the table, and some bubbling coffee, and then, from a hickory-board in front of the fire, took off, with a jerk, brown, flaky slices of Virginia johnny-cake. — MARGRET HOWTH: *Mrs. R. H. Davis.* (*By per.*)

Corn-Meal Flapjacks.

"One quart boiling milk, two cups of white corn-meal. Cook on griddle. Serve rolled, with sugar between."

Corn Bread.

"One quart sour milk, three eggs, two tablespoonfuls butter, one tablespoonful sugar, one-quarter teaspoonful salt, one teacup flour, and enough corn-meal to make a good batter; one teaspoonful soda, or enough to make the milk frothy. Stir thoroughly. Bake in long pans."

Fried Mush.

Into two quarts of boiling water, stir corn-meal, until it makes a smooth mush; boil half an hour; add salt, and stir briskly. Have hot, in a skillet, one tablespoonful each of lard and butter; drop the boiling mush into the skillet in little pats; fry a light crisp brown on both sides.— PRESBYTERIAN COOK-BOOK: *Mrs. W. A. B., Dayton, O.*

Hominy Drop-Cakes.

"One pint of fresh boiled hominy (or cold hominy may be used; if the latter, break into grains, as lightly as possible, with a fork, and heat in a farina-kettle without adding water), one tablespoonful of water, two eggs — whites and yolks beaten separately. Stir the yolks into the hominy first, then the whites, and a teaspoonful of salt if the hominy has not been salted in cooking; or, if it has, use half a teaspoonful. Drop, in tablespoonfuls, on well-buttered tin sheets, and bake to a good brown in a quick oven."

Sally Lunn.

"One quart of flour, butter the size of an egg, three tablespoonfuls of sugar, two eggs, two teacupfuls of milk, two teaspoonfuls of cream-tartar and one of soda, a little salt.

"Stir the sugar, cream-tartar, and salt in the flour, add the eggs without beating, the butter melted, and the milk with the soda dissolved in it."

Rice Waffles.

Rub through a sieve one pint of warm boiled rice; add to it a tablespoonful of dry flour, two-thirds of a teaspoonful of salt, two teaspoonfuls of baking-powder. Beat separately the yolks and whites of three eggs; add to the yolks three gills of milk, work it into the flour, then add an ounce of melted butter; beat the whites of eggs thoroughly; mix the whole together. Heat the waffle-iron, and grease it evenly (a piece of salt pork is best for this purpose); pour the batter into the half of the iron over the range until nearly two-thirds full, cover, allow to cook a moment, then turn and brown slightly on the other side. — *The Cook.* (*By per.*)

Rye Muffins.

Two cups rye, one-half cup of flour, one egg, one-fourth cup molasses, milk to mix quite soft; two scant teaspoons Royal powder sifted with meal and flour. Have your pans very hot before putting in the mixture. — *From* "*Woman's Hour,*" *Boston Globe.* (*By per.*)

Oaten Cakes.

A quarter of a pound of butter to two pounds of oatmeal, then add as much water as will just work them together, but the less the better, and hot water is best; roll them out with a rolling-pin, as thin as possible. One side should be done on the griddle, and the other on the toaster. — DAINTY DISHES: *Lady Harriet St. Clair.*

Frumenty.

Boil wheat till it comes to a jelly, and to a quart of this add, by degrees, two quarts of new milk. Stir and boil till well mixed. Beat the yolks of three eggs with a little nutmeg, and sugar to sweeten it to taste; stir this well in over the fire; pour it into deep dishes, and eat either hot or cold. — DAINTY DISHES: *Lady Harriet St. Clair.*

> I own that I am somewhat of a devotee. I love to keep all festivals, to taste all feast-offerings, from fermety (or frumetry, *frumentum*) at Christmas, to the pancakes at Shrovetide. These things always seem better on those days; as the bread "in the holy days" is ever better than the bread at school, though it come from the same oven. — ESSAYS OF ELIA: *Charles Lamb.*

CHAPTER XIV.

PUDDINGS.

PUDDINGS.

AN APPLE PUDDING.

ONE morning, a little while after our party, mother was making an apple-pudding for dinner, when Madam Pennington and Miss Elizabeth drove round to the door.

Ruth was out at her lessons. Barbara was busy helping Mrs. Holabird. Rosamond went to the door, and let them into the brown room.

"Mother will be sorry to keep you waiting, but she will come directly. She is just in the middle of an apple-pudding."

Rosamond said it with as much simple grace of pride as if she had had to say, "Mother is busy at her modelling, and cannot leave her clay till she has damped and covered it." Her nice perception went to the very farthermost; it discerned the real best to be made of things, the best that was *ready* made, and put that forth.

"And I know," said Madam Pennington, "that an apple-pudding must not be left in the middle. I wonder if she would let an old woman, who has lived in barracks, come to her where she is?"

Rosamond's tact was superlative. She did not say, "I will go and see." She got right up, and said, "I am sure she will; please come this way," and opened the door, with a sublime confidence, full and without warning, upon the scene of operations.

"Oh, how nice!" said Miss Elizabeth; and Madam Pennington walked forward into the sunshine, holding her hand out to Mrs. Holabird, and smiling all the way from her smooth old forehead down to the "seventh beauty" of her dimple-cleft and placid chin.

"Why, this is really coming to see people!" she said.

Mrs. Holabird's white hand did not even want dusting. She just laid down the bright little chopper with which she was reducing her flour and butter to a golden powder, and took Madam Pennington's nicely gloved fingers into her own, without a breath of apology. Apology! It was very meek of her not to look at all set up.

Barbara rose from her chair, with a red ringlet of apple-paring hanging down against her white apron, and seated herself again at her work when the visitors had taken the two opposite corners of the deep, cushioned sofa.

The red cloth was folded back across the end of the dining-table; and at the other end were mother's white board and rolling-pin, the pudding-cloth wrung into a twist out of the scald, and waiting upon a plate, and a pitcher of cold water with ice tinkling against its sides. Mother sat with the deal bowl in her lap, turning and mincing with the few last strokes the light, delicate dust of the pastry. The sunshine — work and sunshine always go so blessedly together — poured in, and filled the room up with life and glory.

"Why, this is the pleasantest room in all your house!" said Miss Elizabeth.

"That is just what Ruth said it would be when we turned it into a kitchen," said Barbara.

"You don't mean that this is really your kitchen!"

"I don't think we are quite sure what it is," replied Barbara, laughing. "We either dine in our kitchen, or kitch in our dining-room; and I don't believe we have found out yet which it is."

"You are wonderful people!"

"You ought to have belonged to the army, and lived in quarters," said Mrs. Pennington. "Only you would have made your rooms so bewitching, you would have been always getting turned out."

"Turned out?"

"Yes; by the ranking family. That is the way they do. The major turns out the captain, and the colonel the major. There's no rest for the sole of your foot till you're a general."

Mrs. Holabird set her bowl on the table, and poured in the icewater. Then the golden dust, turned and cut lightly by the chopper, gathered into a tender, mellow mass, and she lifted it out upon the board. She shook out the scalded cloth, spread it upon the emptied bowl, sprinkled it snowy thick with flour, rolled out the crust with a free quick movement, and laid it on into the curve of the basin. Barbara brought the apples, cut up in white, fresh slices, and slid them into the round. Mrs. Holabird folded over the edges, gathered up the linen cloth in her hands, tied it tightly with a string, and Barbara disappeared with it behind the damask screen, where a puff of steam went up in a minute that told the pudding was in. Then Mrs. Holabird went into the pantry-closet and washed her hands, that never really came to need more than a finger-bowl could do for them, and Barbara carried after her the board and its etceteras, and the red cloth was drawn on again, and there was nothing but a low, comfortable bubble in the chimney-corner to tell of housewifery or dinner.

"I wish it had lasted longer," said Miss Elizabeth. "I am afraid I shall feel like company again now." — WE GIRLS: *Mrs. A. D. T. Whitney. Houghton, Mifflin, & Co., Pubs. (By per.)*

Boiled Apple Pudding.

"Make a butter crust, or a suet one, using for a moderate-sized pudding from three-quarters to one pound of flour, with the other ingredients in proportion. Butter a basin, line it with some of the paste; pare, core, and cut the apples into slices, and fill the basin with these; add sugar to taste, flavor with lemon peel and juice, and cover with crust; pinch the edges together; flour the cloth, place it over the pudding, tie it securely, and put it into plenty of fast-boiling water. Let it boil from one and a half to two and a half hours, according to the size; then turn it out of the basin, and send it to table quickly."

Spanish Fruit Pudding.

Line a baking-dish with a light puff-paste; add a layer of shredded pine-apple, and cover it with powdered sugar; add a layer of sweet oranges sliced; strew over them a thin layer of sugar; next add a layer of sliced bananas with sugar strewn over them. Repeat the process until the dish is full. Cover the dish with a light puff-paste, and bake to a delicate brown. — PUDDINGS AND DAINTY DESSERTS: *Thomas J. Murrey. White, Stokes, & Allen, Pubs.*

Apple Dumplings.

Add to two cups sour milk one teaspoonful soda and one of salt, half cup butter or lard, flour enough to make dough a little stiffer than for biscuit; or, make a good baking-powder crust; peel and core apples; roll out crust, place apples on dough, fill cavity of each with sugar, incase each apple in coating of the crust, press edges tight together (it is nice to tie a cloth around each one), put into kettle of boiling water slightly salted, boil half an hour, taking care that the water covers the dumplings. They are also very nice steamed.

To bake, make in the same way, using a soft dough; place in a shallow pan, bake in a hot oven, and serve with cream and sugar. — EVERY-DAY COOK-BOOK: *Miss Neill. Belford, Clarke, & Co., Pubs.* (*By per.*)

C—— holds that a man cannot have a pure mind who refuses apple-dumplings. I am not certain but he is right. — GRACE BEFORE MEAT: *Charles Lamb.*

Brown Betty.

"Take one cup bread-crumbs, two cups chopped sour apples, one-half cup sugar, one teaspoonful cinnamon, two tablespoonfuls butter cut into small bits. Butter a deep dish, and put a layer of chopped apple at the bottom; sprinkle with sugar, a few bits of butter, and cinnamon; cover with bread-crumbs, then more apple; proceed in this way until the dish is full, having a layer of crumbs on top. Cover closely, and steam three-quarters of an hour in a moderate oven, then uncover and brown quickly. Eat warm with sugar and cream or sweet sauce. This is a cheap but good pudding."

Gateau des Pommes.

"Take a few apples, boil them with as little water as possible, and make them into apple-sauce; then add a pound and a half of sugar, and the juice of a lemon; boil all together till quite firm, and put it into a mould. Garnish it with almonds stuck over it. It will keep for months if allowed to remain in the mould."

Sunday Apple-Sauce.

Core and bake, filling the holes with sugar, seven or eight apples. When very soft, mash them through a sieve into a small pudding-dish; grate in the rind of a fresh lemon, and spread over the top the white of one egg beaten with half a cup of sugar, and brown slightly. Eat cold. — *From " Woman's Hour," Boston Globe. (By per.)*

Rice Meringue.

One cup boiled rice, one large pint milk, two eggs, one large cup sugar, one lemon. Boil the milk, stir in the rice. Beat yolks with one-third of the sugar, then add to the milk and rice, and cook until thick as soft custard. Take from the fire, and grate in rind of lemon ; pour into a buttered dish. Beat whites with the rest of sugar, and add juice of lemon ; pour over pudding, and brown. A delicious pudding. — *From " Woman's Hour," Boston Globe. (By per.)*

Rogrod.

"It is made of the juice, in equal parts, of two fruits, — cherries and currants, or raspberries, — with one-third water, and sugar to suit the taste. Thicken with rice, flour, or sago ; boil, and turn into moulds. Serve with sugar, cream, and powdered cinnamon."

Rice Black-cap Pudding.

"Butter a pudding-basin, stick raisins or prunes all over the bottom, and pour into the centre a teacupful of dry rice, this quantity being sufficient for a basin that will hold a pint of water. Tie a cloth tightly over the basin, and plunge it into boiling water. Boil for an hour, when it will turn out a nice shape, with the raisins or prunes covering the top of the rice, which form the black cap. It can be eaten with sugar and butter, or sirup, or plain pudding-sauce."

Indian-Meal Pudding.

One cup of yellow Indian meal, one quart and a cupful of milk, three eggs, half a cup of molasses, one generous tablespoonful of butter, one teaspoonful of salt, one pint of boiling water, half teaspoonful each of cinnamon and mace. Scald the salted meal with the water. Heat the milk in a farina-kettle; stir in the scalded meal, and boil, stirring often, for half an hour. Beat the eggs light; put in the butter and molasses, stirred together until they are several shades lighter than at first; add the spice; lastly, the batter from the farina-kettle, beaten in a little at a time, until all the ingredients are thoroughly incorporated. Grease a pudding-dish; pour in the mixture, and bake, covered, in a steady oven, three-quarters of an hour. Remove the lid, and brown. This is the genuine, old-fashioned New-England "Indian" pudding. Eat with sauce, or with cream and sugar. It is very nice. — *Marion Harland. The Post, Washington, D.C. (By per.)*

Florentine Pudding.

"Put a quart of milk into your pan, let it come to a boil; mix smoothly three tablespoonfuls of corn-starch and a little cold milk; add the yolks of three eggs beaten, half a teacup of sugar; flavor with vanilla, lemon, or any thing your fancy suggests; stir into the scalding milk, continue stirring till the consistency of starch (ready for use), then put into the pan or dish you wish to serve in. Beat the whites of the eggs with a teacup of pulverized sugar; spread over the top; place it in the oven a few minutes, till the frosting is pretty brown. Can be eaten with cream, or is good enough without. For a change you can bake in cups."

Baked Custards.

"One quart of milk, five eggs, one cup of sugar, and a very little salt. Season with nutmeg, or flavor with rosewater, or any essence preferred. Fill the cups, and set them into a tin of hot water, and bake the custards in a moderate oven. When you think they are done, try them with the handle of a teaspoon inserted at the edge, as they are spoiled by over-baking. Some persons like blanched almonds cut very fine in the custard. If added, use only a little flavor of any other kind."

Amber Pudding.

"Put twelve ounces of finely powdered loaf-sugar, and a pound of butter, into a saucepan; melt the butter, and mix both well: then add the yolks of fifteen eggs well beaten, and as much candied orange, beaten to a fine paste, as will add color and flavor. Line the dish with paste for turning out, fill it up with the above, lay a crust over the top, and bake in a slow oven."

Bread Pudding.

"Take one pint of bread-crumbs soaked in one quart of sweet milk, one-half cup of white sugar, two eggs beaten thoroughly, heaping teaspoonful of butter, and salt to suit the taste; half cup of raisins; stir well together, and bake."

English Tapioca Pudding.

"One cup of tapioca, three pints fresh milk, five eggs, two spoonfuls of butter, one cup of sugar, half pound of raisins seeded and cut in half, half the grated peel of one lemon.

"Soak tapioca one hour in a pint of the milk, pour into jar, and set in a pot of warm water, and bring to a boil. When the tapioca is soft all through, turn out to cool somewhat, while you make the custard. Beat the eggs very light; rub butter and sugar together; mix all with the tapioca, the fruit last. Bake in buttered dish one hour."

Chocolate Pudding.

Add one ounce of grated chocolate to a quart of milk, boil thoroughly, flavor with vanilla; set aside to cool, then stir in the yolks of six eggs well beaten; bake in a buttered pudding-dish until it stiffens like custard. Beat the whites of six eggs, with a table spoonful of powdered sugar, to a stiff froth; spread over the top of the pudding; return to the oven, and brown quickly. — PUDDINGS AND DAINTY DESSERTS: *Thomas J. Murrey. White, Stokes, & Allen, Pubs.*

Strawberry Shortcake.

One cup of powdered sugar, one tablespoonful of butter, three eggs, one rounded cup of prepared flour, two tablespoonfuls of cream, one generous quart of berries. Rub the butter and sugar to a cream, whip in the beaten yolks, the milk, the whites, at last the flour. Bake in three jelly-cake tins, and let the cakes get cold. Cut the berries into halves, and lay between them, sprinkling the strata with sugar. Sift sugar on the topmost layer. Slice, and eat with cream. — *Marion Harland. The Post, Washington, D.C.*

Doubtless God might have made a better berry than the strawberry, but, doubtless, God never did. — *Dr. Boteler.*
We may well celebrate it with festivals and music. It has that indescribable quality of all first things, — that shy, uncloying, provoking, barbed sweetness. It is eager and sanguine as youth. It is born of the copious dews, the fragrant nights, the tender skies, the plentiful rains of the early season. The singing of birds is in it, and the health and frolic of lusty nature. It is the product of liquid May, touched by the June sun. — LOCUSTS AND WILD HONEY: *John Burroughs. Houghton, Mifflin, & Co., Pubs.* (*By per.*)

Compôte of Gooseberries.

Choose a quart of large, sound, ripe, green gooseberries (cost ten cents), remove the stems and tops, throw them into boiling water for two minutes; drain them, let them lie three minutes in cold water containing a tablespoonful of vinegar to restore their color, and then drain them quite dry. Meantime make a thick sirup by boiling one pound of sugar (cost twelve cents) with one pint of water. As soon as the sirup has boiled about ten minutes, put in the gooseberries, and boil them gently until just tender, — about ten minutes. Then pour both fruit and sirup into an earthen or glass dish, cool, and use. The dish will cost less than twenty-five cents. — TWENTY-FIVE-CENT DINNERS: *Miss Juliet Corson. O. Judd Co., Pubs.* (*By per.*)

Blackberry Flummery.

"Stew blackberries, moderately sweetened with sugar, until soft; mix a thickening of flour and water, and stir into the berries. Continue stirring while it boils, until the whole becomes incorporated into a mass just sufficiently thick to pour into moulds; when cold turn out for dessert. To be eaten with milk or cream and sugar."

>Black as Beauty's tresses,
>Sweet as Love's caresses,
>Darlings of the people, beloved of high and low;
>Dear to age and childhood,
>Gleaming in the wildwood,
>Peeping to the sunshine in every green hedgerow;
>Berries of the bramble,
>How I love to ramble
>Through the shady valleys, and pluck you as I go!
>
>BLACKBERRIES: *Charles Mackay.*

Huckleberry Pudding.

One pint of best Orleans molasses; a pinch of salt; one teaspoonful cloves, and one of cinnamon; one of soda dissolved in a teacupful of sweet milk; flour enough to make it the consistency of pound-cake; one quart of huckleberries; boil two and a half hours in a pudding-mould. Eat with cream and sugar, or pudding-sauce. — PRESBYTERIAN COOK-BOOK. *Dayton, O.* (*By per.*)

Roly-Poly.

Take one quart of flour; make good biscuit crust; roll out one-half inch thick, and spread with any kind of fruit, fresh or preserved; fold so that the fruit will not run out; dip cloth into boiling water, and flour it, and lay it around the pudding closely, leaving room to swell; steam one or one and one-half hours; serve with boiled sauce. EVERY-DAY COOK-BOOK: *Miss Neill. Belford, Clarke, & Co., Pubs.* (*By per.*)

English Christmas Plum Pudding.

"One pound of raisins, well stoned; one pound currants, well washed; one-quarter pound suet, finely chopped; one-quarter pound flour, or bread finely crumbled; three ounces of sugar; one ounce and a half of grated lemon-peel, a blade of mace, half a small nutmeg, one teaspoonful of ginger; six eggs, well beaten; work well together; put into a cloth, tie firmly, leaving room to swell, and boil not less than five hours. It should not be allowed to stop boiling."

Cup Plum Pudding.

Take one cup each of raisins, currants, flour, bread-crumbs, suet, and sugar; stone and cut the raisins, wash and dry the currants, chop the suet, and mix all the above ingredients well together; then add two ounces of cut candied peel and citron, a little mixed spice, salt, and ginger, say half a teaspoonful of each; stir in four well-beaten eggs, and milk enough to make the mixture so that the spoon will stand upright in it; tie it loosely in a cloth, or put in a mould; plunge it into boiling water, and boil for three and a half hours. — *Boston Budget.*

Molasses Sauce.

One cupful of molasses, half a cupful of water, one tablespoonful of butter, a little cinnamon or nutmeg (about half a teaspoonful), one-fourth of a teaspoonful of salt, three tablespoonfuls of vinegar.

Boil all together for twenty minutes. The juice of a lemon can be used instead of the vinegar. This sauce is nice for apple or rice puddings. — NEW COOK-BOOK: *Miss Parloa. Estes & Lauriat, Pubs. (By per.)*

Fruit-Sirup Sauce.

One cup fruit-sirup, one-half cup sugar, one teaspoonful corn-starch, one teaspoonful butter. Use the sirup from apricots, peaches, cherries, quinces, or any fruit you prefer. The amount of sugar will depend upon the acidity of the fruit. Mix the corn-starch with the sugar, add the sirup, and boil all together five minutes. Add butter last. — THE PEERLESS COOK-BOOK: *Mrs. D. A. Lincoln. Redding & Co., Pubs. (By per.)*

Hard Sauce.

Beat to a cream a quarter of a pound of butter, add gradually a quarter of a pound of sugar; beat it until very white; add a little lemon-juice, or grate nutmeg on top. — THE EVERY-DAY COOK-BOOK: *Miss Neill. Belford, Clarke, & Co., Pubs. (By per.)*

Foaming Sauce

May be made, all but adding the hot water, a long time before using. Cream half a cupful of butter, add to it one cupful of powdered sugar, then the unbeaten white of one egg, and any flavoring you choose. When the time comes for serving, add slowly an eighth of a cupful of boiling water; then set the bowl into another of hot water, and stir till the sauce is smooth, but not oily, — say about two minutes. — *Public Ledger, Philadelphia. (By per.)*

Plain Pudding-Sauce.

"To three pints of boiling water, add, to thicken, three tablespoonfuls of wheat-flour mixed smooth in a little cold water; put in a tablespoonful, or more, of sugar, a lump of butter, and flavor with nutmeg and essence of lemon or vanilla."

CHAPTER XV.

PIES AND SMALL CAKES.

PIES AND SMALL CAKES.

Murrey's Pie-crust.

It is our firm conviction, that the average pie of to-day is the direct cause of more ill-nature and general "cussedness" in mankind than any thing else, and that there lurks more solid, downright dyspepsia in a square inch of baker's pie than in all the other dyspeptic-producing compounds known. The pie we desire to see upon the American table is one that is more the receptacle for fruit, than a blending of fruit with puff-paste so soggy that lead would digest almost as easily. When a top is used, let there be but little of it, and so light and delicate that "fairy footfalls" would break through it.

Sift together one quart of flour, a teaspoonful of salt, and a tablespoonful of Horsford's baking-powder; add gradually three gills of milk; work to a dough, divide into four parts, and roll out the desired size. This crust when eaten is not harmful. — PUDDINGS AND DAINTY DESSERTS: *Thomas J. Murrey. White, Stokes, & Allen, Pubs.*

Flake Pie-crust.

"Take one-half cup of lard to a pint of flour; rub well together; add water sufficient to make a dough (not too stiff); roll out, and spread with butter, dust with flour, fold over evenly, and roll out again. Repeat this several times (spreading with butter, folding over, and rolling out again). Keep your crust as cold as possible : use ice-water in mixing. Pastry is better when rolled out on marble."

Rhubarb Pie.

Take the tender stalks of rhubarb, strip off the skin, and cut the stalks into thin slices. Line deep plates with pie-crust; then put in the rhubarb, with a thick layer of sugar to each layer of rhubarb; a little grated lemon-peel improves the pie. Cover the pies with a crust, press it down tight upon the edge of the plate, and prick the crust with a fork, so that the crust will not burst while baking, and let out the juices of the pie. Rhubarb-pies should be baked about an hour, in a slow oven : it will not do to bake them quickly. Some cooks stew the rhubarb before making it into pies, but it is not so good as when used without stewing. — AMERICAN HOME COOK-BOOK. *Dick & Fitzgerald, Pubs.* (*By per.*)

Green-Apple Pie.

Stew and strain the apples, and sugar to your taste; grate the peel of a fresh lemon, or flavor with rosewater. Bake in a rich paste half an hour. — *Godey's Lady's Book.* (*By per.*)

Dried-Apple Pie.

To a pint of stewed dried apples, passed through a colander, add a pint of sweet milk, three eggs, and three large tablespoonfuls of sugar, beaten well together as for custard. Spice with a teaspoonful of cinnamon, and half a teaspoonful of ground cloves.

Bake with upper and under crusts. This quantity will make two pies. — *Lizzie Strohm.*

Peach Pies.

Take good ripe peaches, halve and stone them; make a good short crust, and lay it in your pie-plates; lay your peaches evenly to cover it; then add to each moderate-sized pie about three spoonfuls of white sugar, and a few drops of essence of lemon or rose, and half a teacupful of water; cover, and bake like other pies. — *Godey's Lady's Book.*

Prune Pie.

"Stew the prunes until soft, then cool, and remove the stones. Fill your dish with them, sweeten, and spice with a little cinnamon, nutmeg, and cloves. Bake with upper and under crust."

Tomato Pie.

Take ripe tomatoes, wash, peel, and cut in thin slices; fill a pie-dish lined with good paste with them; sprinkle *well* with sugar, and sift a little cinnamon and grated nutmeg over; add two teaspoonfuls of vinegar, and one of lemon-essence; cover with crust, and bake. — *Lulie Strohm.*

Pumpkin Pie.

Wash, cut into halves, and slice a yellow "Yankee pumpkin;" scrape out the seeds and the stringy portions lying next to them, peel, and lay the slices in a steamer over a pot of boiling water. When they can be easily pierced by a fork, take off, and, after emptying the pot of its water, turn the pumpkin into it, and set back on to a moderate fire; leave it uncovered, and stir frequently to prevent scorching, until it seems quite dry, which should be in about fifteen minutes; while hot, press it through a coarse sieve with a potato-masher. Now to one pint of pumpkin take three eggs, the yolks and whites beaten separately; into the yolks stir a small teacup of soft light-brown sugar, half a teaspoonful of cinnamon, and a grate or two of nutmeg; if ginger is preferred as a flavoring, a very scant teaspoonful may be used, and half a teaspoonful of salt. Stir this to a cream, mix with the pumpkin, and add a quart of milk; beat the whites of the eggs, and stir all well together. Do not have the crust too short, else there will be trouble in getting the pie from the pan. Roll quite thin, bake well in the bottom, and remove from the oven when the pie is firm in the centre. This will result in a pumpkin pie "fit to set before the king." — *Commercial Gazette, Cincinnati, O.* (*By per.*)

Ah! on Thanksgiving Day, when from East and from West,
From North and from South, come the pilgrim and guest,
When the gray-haired New-Englander sees round his board
The old broken links of affection restored,
When the care-wearied man seeks his mother once more,
And the worn matron smiles where the girl smiled before,
What moistens the lip, and what brightens the eye,
What calls back the past, like the rich pumpkin pie?

THE PUMPKIN: *J. G. Whittier.* (*By per. Houghton, Mifflin, & Co.*)

Squash Pie.

"One cup stewed squash, one-half cup of sugar, two eggs, and milk enough to fill pie-plate. First line pie-plate with crust, then beat eggs and sugar together, adding squash and milk. Season with cinnamon, nutmeg, and allspice, to suit the taste. Bake till well done."

Custard Pie.

"Take three eggs beaten thoroughly, two heaping tablespoonfuls of white sugar, one pint of milk, nutmeg to suit the taste, and a little salt; stir all together, adding the eggs last."

Cream Pies.

"Make the crust as usual, and spread on the tins. For each pie take one-half cup of pulverized sugar and nearly as much of sifted flour; rub together dry, and spread over the crust. (It is quite essential that the flour and sugar should be well mixed before uniting with the cream, as it prevents all possibility to lumps.) Pour over it one cup of sour cream, and a few spoonfuls of sour or loppered milk, stir gently into the flour and sugar. Grate over a little nutmeg, and bake in quick oven. It is better to place an iron grate in the oven under the pies, as they are liable to 'run over' if too hot at the bottom. These pies are always in good demand. If sweet cream is used, no milk should be added. They should always be eaten fresh, but are good cold or warm."

Cocoanut Pies.

One cocoanut grated, four eggs, one-half cup butter, two and one-half cups sugar, one pint milk. If the desiccated cocoanut is used, take two and one-half cups, and soak in milk two or three hours. — "*Woman's Hour,*" *Sunday Globe, Boston, Mass.* (*By per.*)

Lemon Pie. No. 1.

"Take juice and grated rind of one lemon; stir together with three-fourths of a cup of white sugar and one cup of water; lastly, stir in four eggs, well beaten, reserving the whites of two for frosting. Fill into crust, and bake. For frosting beat the whites of two eggs reserved, to a stiff froth, with a tablespoonful of powdered sugar; spread over the top evenly, and return to oven until slightly browned."

Lemon Pie. No. 2.

"To one lemon cut in thin slices, add one teacupful of sugar, and a tablespoonful of flour mixed with the sugar. Fill up with water, and bake slowly."

Orange Pie. No. 1.

"One orange grated, five crackers rolled fine, a pint of sweet milk, two eggs well beaten, sugar to sweeten. Bake as custard."

Orange Pie. No. 2.

"Make a cake of one and a half cups of sugar, one-half cup of butter, two-thirds of a cup of milk, two cups of flour, three eggs; one teaspoonful of cream-tartar in the flour, one-half teaspoonful of soda in the milk. Flavor with the juice and grated rind of an orange. Bake it in low tins as for Washington pie. When cool, add the juice of two oranges, and the grated rind of one orange, mixed with sufficient granulated sugar to thicken and sweeten it; spread this like jelly between the layers of the cake. Frost, if you like, with the white of one egg, a small cup of sugar, and flavor with orange."

Raisin Pie.

"One lemon, juice and yellow rind; one cup of raisins, one cup water, one cup rolled crackers, one cup of sugar. Stone the raisins, and boil in water to soften."

Mincemeat without Brandy.

Take six pounds of beef from the shoulder, and boil fast for a few moments so as to seal up the pores of the meat; then more slowly until quite tender, salting as if for table use. Allow it to simmer down as dry as possible without scorching, thereby saving all the juice of the meat. If this is not successfully done, use the liquor which is left, in the mincemeat. It must be perfectly cold before chopping. To every pint of meat take three cups of chopped apple. If the pies are preferred cold, use, instead of suet, two pints of melted butter; otherwise, one-half the quantity of butter and one pound of finely chopped suet will do; the juice of three lemons; three pints of brown sugar (if this quantity does not sweeten sufficiently, add cautiously to suit the taste); three pounds of raisins, the largest of them cut in two and seeded; two pounds of well-washed currants; two gallons of sweet cider (if it has fermented, add another half-gallon, and boil in a granite or porcelain kettle an hour and a half); two heaping teaspoonfuls of cinnamon, one level spoonful each of cloves and pepper, two small nutmegs, and, if citron is liked, one-half pound cut into small pieces. It should be mixed one day at least before using, and will keep two weeks in cold weather; or it may be heated thoroughly and canned. If more spices are liked, they can be added: better not enough than too much. — *Commercial Gazette, Cincinnati, O.* (*By per.*)

I was happy to find my old friend, minced-pie, in the retinue of the feast; and finding him to be perfectly orthodox, and that I need not be ashamed of my predilection, I greeted him with all the warmth wherewith we usually greet an old and very genteel acquaintance. — THE SKETCH-BOOK: CHRISTMAS EVE: *Washington Irving.* (*By per. G. P. Putnam's Sons.*)

Editor's Doughnuts.

"One cup of sugar, one of buttermilk, one teaspoonful of soda dissolved in the milk, one egg, tablespoonful of lard, one-fourth of a nutmeg, and a little cinnamon; flour to make stiff enough to roll. Cut in shapes, and drop into boiling lard; when taken out and partly cool, dip in powdered sugar."

Crullers.

"One cup of sugar, two eggs, one large spoonful of butter, two and a half spoonfuls baking-powder, flour sufficient to roll, flavor to taste. Fry as doughnuts."

Sour-Cream Cookies.

"One cup of sour cream, one cup of sugar, two eggs, one teaspoonful (not heaping) of soda, a little salt, and flour enough to make a soft dough; flavor with caraway-seeds."

Jumbles.

"One cup of butter, two cups of sugar, one cup of milk, four eggs, one teaspoonful soda, six cups flour, a little nutmeg. Roll them out, cut them with a tumbler and a wine-glass to form a ring; dust over with the white of an egg, and sift on a little sugar before baking."

Ginger-Snaps.

"One pint of molasses, one-half pound sugar, two tablespoonfuls ginger, one teaspoonful of cinnamon, half pound of butter. Mix well, and roll thin."

Soft Gingerbread.

"Half pint of buttermilk, half pint molasses, half teacup butter, teaspoonful of soda dissolved in hot water, one tablespoonful of ginger, teaspoonful cinnamon, and half a nutmeg. Stir in flour until it is a thick batter. Bake in square pans half an hour."

Ginger Horse-Cakes.

"One quart of flour, one pint of best Orleans molasses, one cupful of sugar, tablespoonful and a half of ginger, two small teaspoonfuls of soda, half a cupful of sour cream, and a heaping tablespoonful of lard. Sift the flour first, and then sprinkle the ginger well through it; add the sugar and molasses, putting in lastly the soda dissolved in the cream. Obtain from a tinner a cutter shaped like a horse, for cutting out the cakes."

Rock Cakes.

Mix well together four ounces each of butter and sugar (cost twelve cents); add four ounces of well-washed currants (cost three cents), one pound of flour (cost four cents), and three eggs (cost three cents); beat all these ingredients thoroughly; roll them into little balls, or rocks, and bake them on a buttered baking-pan. A good supply will cost about twenty-two cents. — TWENTY-FIVE-CENT DINNERS: *Miss Juliet Corson. O. Judd Co., Pubs. (By per.)*

CHAPTER XVI.

CAKES, DESSERTS, ICE-CREAMS, TEA, COFFEE, CHOCOLATE.

CAKES, DESSERTS, ICE-CREAMS, TEA, COFFEE, CHOCOLATE.

THE PARTY.

DONALD and Dorry joined the merry line, wondering what was about to happen — when, to their great surprise (ah, that sly Uncle George, and that innocent Liddy!), the double doors leading into the dining-room were flung open, and there, sparkling in the light of a hundred wax candles, was a collation fit for Cinderella and all her royal court. I shall not attempt to describe it, for fear of forgetting to name some of the good things. Imagine what you will, and I do believe there was something just like it, or quite as good, upon that delightful table, so beautiful with its airy, fairy-like structures of candied fruits, frostings, and flowers; its jagged rock of ice where chickens and turtles, made of ice-cream, were resting on every peak and cranny; its gold-tinted jellies, and its snowy temples. . . . At this very moment, Gory Danby, quite unconscious of the feast upstairs, was having his own private table in the kitchen. Having grown hungry for his usual supper of bread and milk, he had stolen in upon Norah, and begged for it so charmingly, that she was unable to resist him. Imagine his surprise when, drowsily taking his last mouthful, he saw Fandy rush into the room with a plate of white grapes.

"Gory Danby!" exclaimed that disgusted brother, "I'm 'shamed of you! What you stuffin' yourse'f with common supper for when there's *a party* upstairs? Splendid things, all made of sugar! Pull off that bib now, an' come along!" — DONALD AND DOROTHY· *Mrs. Mary Mapes Dodge. Roberts Bros., Pubs.* (*By per.*)

Angel Cake.

The whites of eleven eggs, one and a half cupfuls of granulated sugar; one cupful of pastry-flour, measured after being sifted four times; one teaspoonful of cream of tartar, one of vanilla extract. Sift the flour and cream of tartar together. Beat the whites to a stiff froth. Beat the sugar into the eggs, and add the seasoning and flour, stirring quickly and lightly. Beat until ready to put the mixture in the oven. Use a pan that has little legs at the top corners, so that when the pan is turned upside down on the table, after the baking, a current of air will pass under and over it. Bake for forty minutes in a moderate oven. Do not grease the pan. — NEW COOK-BOOK: *Miss Maria Parloa. Estes & Lauriat, Pubs.* (*By per.*)

Silver Cake.

The whites of five eggs, one cup of sugar, two and one-half cups of flour, one-half cup of butter, one-half cup of milk; one teaspoonful of cream-tartar, and one-half teaspooonful of soda. Mix the butter and sugar together; add the milk, then the flour in which has been mixed the cream-tartar, then the whites of the eggs; then the soda, dissolved in a little boiling water. — PRESBYTERIAN COOK-BOOK. *Dayton, O.* (*By per.*)

Gold Cake.

One cup of butter, two cups of sugar, three cups of flour, one-half a cup of milk, the yolks of five eggs; one teaspoonful of cream-tartar, one-half teaspoonful of soda; flavor to taste. — PRESBYTERIAN COOK-BOOK. *Dayton, O.* (*By per.*)

Marble Cake.

Light part: Whites of seven eggs, three cups of white sugar, one of butter, one of milk, four of flour; one and one-half teaspoonfuls of baking-powder.

Dark part: Yolks of seven eggs, two cupfuls of

brown sugar, one of butter, one of milk, one of Orleans molasses, and four of flour; one tablespoonful of baking-powder, one of cinnamon, one of allspice, and one-half tablespoonful of cloves. Put some of the white mixture first into the pan, then with a large spoon drop in some of the dark, alternating until all is used. This will make one large and one small cake. — PRESBYTERIAN COOK-BOOK: *Miss J. A. E.*

Hickory-Nut Cake.

"One cup broken hickory-nut meats, one and one-half cup sugar, one-half cup butter, two cups flour, three-fourths cup sweet milk; two teaspoonfuls baking-powder, and the whites of four eggs well beaten; flavor with vanilla. Add the meats last."

Watermelon Cake.

White part: Two cups of sugar, one-half cup of butter, one of sweet milk, two teaspoonfuls of baking-powder, two and one-half cups of flour, and one lemon.

Pink part: Made the same as the white, except use pink sugar (which can be bought at the confectioners), and one-half pound of raisins. Put the raisins in the sugar. Put the pink part all in the centre of the pan, and the white on the outside. — PRESBYTERIAN COOK-BOOK: *Mrs. Graham.*

Pound Cake.

One pound of sugar, three-quarters of a pound of butter, one of flour, nine eggs; a piece of sal-volatile the size of a pea, dissolved in a teaspoonful of water.

Beat butter and sugar to a cream; then add the eggs beaten separately, lastly the flour. — PRESBYTERIAN COOK-BOOK: *Miss P.*

Éclairs.

Put in a saucepan half a pound of butter; whisk into it a quart of boiled milk, and add gradually one pound of sifted flour, and a saltspoonful of salt. Stir the milk briskly with a wooden spoon, while the flour is being added; allow the paste to stand on the range a few minutes to evaporate some of its moisture; then add one egg at a time, beating thoroughly, until the paste shows signs of becoming sticky instead of being smooth.

No definite number of eggs can be prescribed to attain this result, as there is so much difference in flour; but from five to seven will be sufficient to produce the desired consistency. Put the paste in a funnel-shaped bag, having a tin tube in the small end, and squeeze it out on a buttered pan, making the éclair three or four inches long. Then bake these forms of light paste for about twenty minutes.

Prepare a cream as follows: Put two quarts of milk on the range, and add to it half a pound of powdered sugar. Put together a quarter of a pound of flour, and four eggs, and one vanilla-bean; beat thoroughly; when the milk boils, add it to the flour and eggs, and whisk lively. Set the mixture on the range; let it come to a boil, and pour it into a bowl to become cold. When cold, stir into this cream a pint of whipped cream.

Cut the éclairs on the side, and fill them with the cream. They may be served plain or with a covering of chocolate, icing, or coffee *fondant.* — PUDDINGS AND DAINTY DESSERTS: *Thomas J. Murrey.* White, Stokes, & Allen, Pubs.

Lady-Fingers.

One cup sugar, three tablespoons milk, one egg, one teaspoon cream-tartar, three tablespoons melted butter, nutmeg, one even teaspoon soda.

Mix with flour to roll out thin, sprinkle powdered sugar over, and cut in long thin strips. Bake quickly. — THE PEERLESS COOK-BOOK: *Mrs. D. A. Lincoln.* (*By per.*)

Sponge Cake. No. 1.

"One cup of pulverized sugar, one cup of flour, one-third cup of sweet milk, three eggs, one teaspoonful of cream of tartar, one-half teaspoonful of soda. Beat the whites and yolks of the eggs separately and thoroughly; add the whites *last.* Mix, and bake in a hot oven."

Sponge Cake. No. 2.

"One teacup of flour, one of pulverized sugar, teaspoonful of baking-powder, three eggs well beaten; flavor with essence."

Dried-Apple Cake.

Two cups of sweet dried apples, soak over night, and chop; add two cups of molasses, and let it simmer two hours; when cold add one cup of sugar, two eggs, one-half cup each of sour cream, sour milk, and butter; two teaspoonfuls of soda, four cups of flour, four teaspoonfuls of cinnamon, one teaspoonful of cloves, and one nutmeg. — *Exchange.*

Jelly Fruit Cake.

"Two cups of sugar, two-thirds cup butter, one cup sweet milk, three cups of flour, three eggs, one teaspoonful baking-powder. Flavor with lemon. Bake one-half of the above mixture in two pans. To the remainder add one teaspoonful molasses, one cup of raisins, one-half cup currants, and piece of citron chopped fine. Bake in two tins. Put the four layers together alternately with frosting and jelly."

Jelly for Cake.

"One quart of cranberries, and one pound of brown sugar. Cook as for table use; then strain through sieve, and let jelly."

Black Cake.

One pound butter, one pound sugar, beaten to a cream; stir in twelve eggs, beaten well; sift in one pound flour; add three pounds stoned raisins, three pounds cleaned currants, five nutmegs, one-half ounce cinnamon, one teaspoonful cloves, one pound citron cut in small thin slices; these must be well mixed; bake in a moderate oven. This improves by keeping. — *Peterson's Magazine.* (*By per.*)

Cocoanut Cakes.

"Half pound of pounded sugar to a large cocoanut grated, put into a preserving-pan till the sugar melts. Form into cakes; put on white paper. They should be well baked in a very cool oven, and when cooked ought to be pure white."

Macaroons.

"Blanch and beat half a pound of sweet almonds in a mortar with a spoonful of water till quite fine, gradually adding the whites of eight eggs, whisked or beaten to a froth; then mix in half a pound of loaf-sugar finely powdered. Spread sheets of white paper on your baking-tin, and over that the proper wafer-paper. Lay the paste on it in pieces about the size of a walnut, and sift fine sugar over. Bake carefully in a moderately hot oven, and when cold cut the wafer-paper round. If you choose, you can lay two or three almond-strips on the top of each cake as they begin to bake."

Dents de Loup Biscuit.

Fold two sheets of paper lengthwise like a fan, then double it, butter the paper, and spread it open. Break into a pan two eggs, and mix with them four spoonfuls of powdered sugar, two of flour, and the grated rinds of two lemons; and when these are well mixed together, add a quarter pound of melted butter. Pour a spoonful of this preparation on the edge of the paper, guiding it along the folds with your finger; take another spoonful, and do the same, leaving a space between the folds, that they may not touch in baking. Sprinkle them with sugared anise-seed, or any other spice preferred, and bake them in a well-heated oven, and as soon as they are taken out, shake them from the paper carefully, that they may not break."

Dominoes.

Have any kind of sponge-cake, baked in a rather thin sheet. Cut this into small, oblong pieces, the shape of a domino. Frost the top and sides of them. When the frosting is hard, draw the black lines, and make the dots, with a small brush that has been dipped in melted chocolate. — NEW COOK-BOOK: *Miss Maria Parloa. Estes & Lauriat, Pubs.* (*By per.*)

Bachelor Buttons.

These delicious little cakes are prepared by rubbing two ounces of butter into five ounces of flour; add five ounces of white sugar; beat an egg with half the sugar, then put it to the other ingredients; add almond flavoring according to taste. Roll them in the hand about the size of a large nut, sprinkle them with white sugar, and place them on tins with buttered paper. They should be slightly baked. — *Godey's Lady's Book.* (*By per.*)

Maids of Honor.

Make some new milk lukewarm, then put in a spoonful of rennet, and stir it well through a cheese-cloth to get rid of the whey; to half a pound of the curd put six ounces of butter, four yolks of eggs, and sugar and nutmeg to taste. Mix all the ingredients well; line patty-pans with a puff paste, fill them with the mixture, and bake in a quick oven. The cheese-cakes may be flavored with lemon if desired. — *Peterson's Magazine.* (*By per.*)

Bow-Knots.

Cut thin puff-paste into half-inch strips, and shape them on the baking-pan into the form of a double bow-knot. When baked, put jelly on each loop of the bow. — BOSTON COOK-BOOK: *Mrs. D. A. Lincoln. Roberts Brothers, Pubs. (By per.)*

Cupid's Wells.

Cut the rounds of puff-paste of three or four different sizes; use the largest one for the bottom, and cut the centres from the others, leaving the rims of different widths, and put them on the whole round, with the narrowest at the top. Bake, and fill with jelly. — THE BOSTON COOK-BOOK: *Mrs. D. A. Lincoln. Roberts Brothers, Pubs. (By per.)*

Rich Bride-Cake.

Take four pounds of fine flour, dry it; four pounds of sweet, fresh butter, beaten to a cream; and two pounds of white sugar; add six eggs to every pound of flour; mace and nutmeg, half an ounce each, pound them fine. Wash through several waters, and pick clean, four pounds of currants; spread them on a thickly folded cloth to dry; stone and chop four pounds of raisins, cut two pounds of citron in slices of a quarter of an inch thickness, and chop or cut in slices one pound of almonds. Beat the yolks of the eggs with the sugar to a smooth paste; beat the butter and flour together, and add them to the yolks and sugar; and, lastly, add the spices, and the whites of the eggs beaten to a high froth. Beat the cake mixture well together; then stir into it, by degrees, the currants, citron, raisins, and almonds. Butter the pans, line them with paper, and put the mixture two inches deep in each. Bake according to the depth of the cakes, three or four hours, in a moderate oven. — *Godey's Lady's Book.* (*By per. Pub.*)

Twelfth-Night Cake.

Take one cup butter, two of sugar, three and a half of flour, one of milk, yolks of five eggs, whites of three, three teaspoonfuls of baking-powder, one of orange-extract, one pea, one bean, one clove.

In making cake, as in every thing else, it is necessary to have every thing ready. Have a round pan with a tube in the middle. Take sheets of unglazed white, paper, and butter them; cut a hole for the tube, and place in the pan, lining it thoroughly. When the cake is done, it can be lifted out by this paper. Have butter, milk, and flour measured out, and eggs broken and separated. Mix the baking-powder into the flour.

Then, in cold weather always fill the bowl in which you are to mix cake, with hot water; let it stand a moment, and then pour out. This heats the bowl enough to warm the butter, which must not be melted. Mix with your hand, or a spoon, as you please; you will find it much easier to mix with the hand.

Rub the butter to a soft smooth cream, and add the flour with the flavoring extract gradually. Beat very light. Meanwhile have the eggs beaten, the whites first, and then the yolks. The butter and sugar must be rubbed together till very light. Use a fine granulated sugar for this. Add the milk, a little at a time, and rub and mix to keep it smooth. If the whole cupful should be added at once, the mixture would be separated into a whey-like substance, and the consequence would be a coarse-grained cake. If inclined to separate, add a little flour to stop it.

In making cake, be sure to make it as quickly as possible.

Add the flour, with the baking-powder in it, and beat up quickly; then the well-beaten yolks, then the whites beaten stiff. Scrape down with a knife from the sides of the bowl, so there will be no hard lumps in the cake. Pour the dough into the pan, and set into the oven. Have a quick heat at first, especially from the bottom. It should rise so as to fill the pan.

When the cake is done, and before it is frosted, push into it on one side the pea, and on the other the bean and the clove. Mark with a broom-straw, so you will remember where you put these. Then ice and decorate the loaf.

When the cake is cut, gentlemen must be served from the side containing the clove and bean, and the ladies from the side containing the pea, according to the ancient custom. The clove represents the knave, the bean is the king, and the pea is the queen. Those to whom these fall in the cutting of the cake must assume the characters represented by them for the evening. This is an ancient English custom, which has been revived of late years.

A wreath of angelica leaves and red cherries about the edge is a pretty decoration, and in the centre should be placed a tiny Christmas-tree. Have little figures of a king, queen, and knave made at a confectioner's, and place them on top of the cake. — *Mrs. Daniell:* (No. 5) *Boston Cooking School. From Boston Globe.* (*By per.*)

Plain Frosting.

Place the whites of one, two, or more eggs in a bowl. Throw into them a tablespoonful of pulverized white sugar; that known as "confectioner's" sugar is the best. Beat with a wooden spoon, adding sugar by the spoonful, and beating well between the additions. It is impossible to state the exact amount of sugar, as the size and freshness of eggs vary so much; but use about one cupful of sugar for one white of an egg. If, when drawing the end of a knife-blade through the frosting on the back of a spoon, it leaves a clean-cut line, consider the frosting sufficiently beaten.

It is best to frost cake while it is warm. Spread first over the cake a thin coating of the frosting, with a long, thin knife. This fills the pores, and the heat of the cake melts the sugar, causing the frosting to cling very securely. Next put on with a spoon sufficient to cover the cake, spreading evenly over the whole surface. After smoothing, mark where it is to be cut, and set in a cool place to harden. Lemon-juice is the nicest flavoring, making the frosting light, and may be used to thin frosting which spreads too stiff. This may be kept a few days, if covered very closely from the air. — *Mrs. Daniell:* (No. 5) *Boston Cooking School. From Boston Globe.* (*By per.*)

To stone Raisins easily.

Pour boiling water over them, letting them stand a moment to soften, then pour it off. The stones may then be easily pinched out at the stem end by giving an "extra twist" to the fruit. — *Public Ledger, Philadelphia.*

Charlotte Russe.

Whip one quart rich cream to a stiff froth, and drain well on a nice sieve. To one scant pint of milk add six eggs beaten very light; make very sweet; flavor high with vanilla. Cook over hot water till it is a thick custard. Soak one full ounce Cox's gelatine in a very little water, and warm over hot water. When the custard is very cold, beat in lightly the gelatine and the whipped cream. Line the bottom of your mould with buttered paper, the sides with sponge-cake or lady-fingers fastened together with the white of an egg. Fill with the cream; put in a cold place, or in summer on ice. To turn out, dip the mould for a moment in hot water. In draining the whipped cream, all that drips through can be re-whipped. — THE EVERY-DAY COOK-BOOK: *Miss Neill.* (*By per. Belford, Clarke, & Co.*).

Raspberry Blancmange.

Three pints raspberries, one ounce and a half gelatine, one pint cream, one-half pound loaf-sugar.

Put the fruit into an enamelled preserving-pan, and bruise it a little with a wooden spoon, then set the pan on the side of the fire where the juice may be drawn slowly from the berries. Have the gelatine soaked for an hour in half a cup of cold water. Then strain the juice from the raspberries, and put it into the pan together with the sugar and the gelatine, and let the whole boil gently until the gelatine is dissolved. Add, very gradually, the cream, stirring it in well. Have ready a dampened mould, pour the blancmange into it, and place it on the ice. When set, it is ready to turn out and serve. — *The Caterer.* (*By per.*)

Floating Island.

Put a quart of milk on to boil; meanwhile beat to a stiff froth the whites of four eggs, and when the milk is just boiling put them in it, stir once or twice, and then *immediately* lift out. Use a ladle with holes in, that the milk may not be taken out with the frothed whites. Have ready the yolks well beaten; add to them a tablespoonful of corn-starch mixed smoothly with a little milk, and sweeten all to taste. After removing the whites from the milk, put in the yolks and corn-starch, and let all just come to the boil. Flavor with vanilla or any essence preferred. Take off, and pour in a deep glass dish, and place upon the top the frothed whites. — *Miss Lizzie Strohm.*

Lemon Snow.

Soak one ounce of gelatine (cost eight cents) in one pint of cold water for half an hour; peel the yellow rind from three lemons (cost six cents), and squeeze and strain their juice; put the rind and juice of the lemons into a saucepan with eight ounces of loaf-sugar (cost eight cents), and stir until the sugar and gelatine are quite dissolved; pour it into a bowl, and let it it cool, and begin to grow firm. Then add the whites of three eggs (cost three cents), and beat to a stiff froth. Pile by the tablespoonful high in the centre of a glass dish. It is pretty and delicious, and costs only about twenty-five cents. — TWENTY-FIVE-CENT DINNERS: *Miss Juliet Corson.* (*By per.*)

Orange Baskets.

Cut as many oranges as will be required, leaving half the peel whole for the baskets, and a strip half an inch wide for the handle. Remove the pulp and juice, and use the juice in making orange-jelly. Place the baskets in a pan of broken ice to keep upright. Fill with *orange-jelly.* When ready to serve, put *a spoonful* of *whipped cream* over the jelly in each basket. Serve in a bed of *orange* or *laurel leaves.* — THE BOSTON COOK-BOOK: *Mrs. D. A. Lincoln. Roberts Brothers, Pubs.* (*By per.*)

Ambrosia.

"Peel and cut up a dish of oranges, removing all the tough skin and seeds. Cover a layer of orange with sugar and grated cocoanut, and proceed in this way until the dish is filled. Cover the top with the sugar and cocoanut."

Ice-Cream, Lemon or Vanilla.

"One quart of cream, one pint of milk, cup and a half of sugar, flavor with large tablespoonful essence of lemon or vanilla. Beat the cream to a froth; stir in the milk and sugar thoroughly; flavor, freeze, and pack for two hours."

Strawberry Ice-Cream.

Sprinkle two cups of sugar over two quarts of strawberries. Mash them, and let them stand half an hour, or until the sugar is dissolved; and meanwhile prepare the ice, and pack the freezer. Turn the berries into a large square of cheese-cloth, placed over a bowl, and squeeze as long as any juice or pulp will come. Then empty the pulp and seeds left in the cloth into a pan, and pour on gradually about a pint of milk; mix it well with the pulp, until the pulp is separated from the seeds. Squeeze again until perfectly dry. There should be nothing left in the cloth save a ball of seeds. Add to the juice as much cream as you may have, from one cup to three pints, and sugar to make it very sweet. Freeze as usual. After tasting this, you will never want any other strawberry ice-cream. — THE PEERLESS COOK-BOOK: *Mrs. D. A. Lincoln. Redding & Co., Pubs.* (*By per.*)

Peach Ice-Cream.

"Pare and cut in small pieces one dozen peaches, or more if desired, and boil them with half a pound of loaf-sugar. When reduced to a marmalade, press them through a fine sieve. When cool add one pint of cream, and a few drops of cochineal to give a deeper peach-color. Freeze. Serve with halves or quarters of fresh peaches half frozen around the cream."

Coffee Cream.

Take very rich cream, beat it well, and sweeten very sweet with powdered loaf-sugar. Prepare in the best manner a decoction of very strong coffee; it must be very clear; stir sufficient into the cream to flavor it highly, and freeze; it will be a darkish color, but is highly esteemed by gentlemen. — *Peterson's Magazine.* (*By per.*)

Chocolate Ice-Cream.

Scrape up a quarter of a pound of Baker's chocolate, and dissolve it in a little water; then add to it one quart of fresh milk, and put it on the fire in a stewpan to boil, stirring it all the time. Make a paste of a tablespoonful of corn-starch and the same quantity of cold milk; stir it into the chocolate, and boil until it has well thickened, which should be in about fifteen minutes; add two teacupfuls of white sugar, and a teaspoonful of vanilla-extract; when well thickened, remove the chocolate from the fire, and add it to a quart of rich cream. Freeze as usual. — VIRGINIA COOKERY-BOOK: *Mrs. Mary Stuart Smith.* (*By per.*) *Harper & Brothers, Pubs.*

Tutti Frutti.

One gallon of cream, one can of peaches, one can of apricots, six lemons, six oranges, twelve bananas. Chop the peaches and apricots; add the juice of the lemons and oranges, with the pulp of three of each; whip the cream thoroughly, having first sweetened it to your taste, and stir into the fruit. Two pounds will probably be about the quantity of sugar required. Freeze all together to a paste; then add the bananas, cutting them up into quarter-inch slices with a silver knife; stir them in lightly with a *silver* spoon, and complete the freezing. This quantity makes two gallons when frozen. — VIRGINIA COOKERY-BOOK: *Mrs. Mary Stuart Smith. Harper & Brothers, Pubs.* (*By per.*)

Salted Almonds.

Shell the almonds, and blanch by throwing them into boiling water, and leaving them there, covered, for half an hour, or until the skins will slip off easily. Skin, and spread them out to dry for several hours. Put a good piece of butter into a hot dripping-pan, and as it warms stir the almonds over and over in it to coat them with the butter. Set in the oven, and roast, stirring them often until they begin to color faintly. Take them out, shake in a colander to rid of grease, spread on a dish, and strew with fine dry salt, stirring them about that each nut may have its share. Eat cold. They are charmingly appetizing. Avoid the dangers of getting the almonds too brown, and, on the other hand, of putting them into the oven before they are dry enough. — *Brooklyn Times.*

After-Dinner Croûtons.

The hard water-crackers being expensive in comparison with other crackers, I have adopted the crispy *croûtons* as a substitute, and find them very acceptable. Cut sandwich-bread into slices one-quarter of an inch thick; cut each slice into four small triangles; dry them in the oven slowly until they assume a delicate brownish tint, then serve either hot or cold. A nice way to serve them is to spread a paste of part butter and part rich creamy cheese, to which may be added a very little minced parsley. — PUDDINGS AND DAINTY DESSERTS: *Thomas J. Murrey. White, Stokes, & Allen, Pubs.*

Candied Cherries.

Choose a pound of perfectly sound, ripe cherries (cost ten cents), with the stalks and an occasional leaf attached; wipe them with a clean, dry, soft cloth; dip the leaves and stems, but not the fruit, into boiling vinegar, and set them, with the cherries upward, in a cardboard perforated with holes to admit the stems, until the vinegar dries. Meantime, boil a pound of loaf-sugar (cost about fifteen cents) with a teaspoonful of cold water, using a thick, porcelain-lined saucepan or copper sugar-boiler; skim until perfectly clear, and test in the following way: Dip the thumb and forefinger into cold water, and then quickly into the boiling sugar, withdrawing it instantly; press the fingers together, and then draw them apart: if the sugar forms a little thread between them, it is ready to use; if it does not, boil a few minutes longer, and test again. When it is ready, dip the leaves and branches into it, and dry them in the cardboard frame as directed above. Keep the sugar at the boiling-point, and as soon as it forms a clear, brittle thread between the fingers when tested as above, dip the entire fruit into it, moving the cherries around so that the sugar completely covers them; and dry them, placed as above in the cardboard frame, in the mouth of a cool oven. — TWENTY-FIVE-CENT DINNERS: *Miss Juliet Corson. O. Judd Co., Pubs.* (*By per.*)

Iced Currants.

Beat the white of one egg (cost one cent) to a stiff froth, mix it with three dessertspoonfuls of cold water; dip into it carefully some perfect bunches of ripe red and white currants, which can be bought in season for ten cents a pound; drain each bunch a moment, and then dust it well with powdered sugar; lay each bunch carefully upon a large sheet of white paper, so that there is plenty of room between the bunches, and set them in a cool, airy place for five hours. The sugar will partly crystallize upon the fruit, and the effect will be very pretty. The cost of a good-sized dish will be about fifteen cents. TWENTY-FIVE-CENT DINNERS: *Miss Juliet Corson.* O. Judd Co., Pubs. (*By per.*)

Orange Water Ice.

Take as many oranges as will be necessary, cut them in half, and press the juice from them; take the pulp carefully from the rind, and put it in a bowl, pour a little boiling water on it, stir it well, and strain it through a sieve; mix this with the orange-juice, and stir in as much sugar as will make a rich sirup. If the oranges are fine, rub some of the sugar on the peel to extract the essence. Freeze it like ice-cream. — *Godey's Lady's Book.* (*By per.*)

Grape Sherbet.

Lay a square of cheese-cloth over a bowl; put in a pound of ripe Concord grapes; mash very thoroughly with a wooden masher. Squeeze out all the juice; add an equal amount of cold water, the juice of one lemon, and sugar to make it very sweet. Freeze as usual. — THE PEERLESS COOK-BOOK : *Mrs. D. A. Lincoln. Redding & Co., Pubs.* (*By per.*)

To make Tea.

Put the tea in a perfectly clean and dry teapot ten minutes or a quarter of an hour before it is required; warm both the pot and the tea by placing them in the oven or before the fire; then fill the teapot with boiling water, allow it to stand for five minutes, and it is ready. — *Sayer.*

"This method improves the fragrance of the tea very considerably, slightly but pleasantly altering the flavor; it appears to act by removing any trace of moisture or dampness from the tea, and by developing the aromatic principle."

Iced Tea.

Make the tea in the usual way; do not let it get cold on the leaves, but strain it off at the end of ten minutes after the boiling water is poured on, and set aside to cool. In using it, put two or three lumps of sugar in a glass, half fill it with broken ice, pour in the tea, and stir rapidly until the sugar melts. It is a delicious and refreshing beverage. — *Marion Harland. The Post, Washington, D.C.* (*By per.*)

To boil Coffee.

Grind a teacupful of coffee in the evening, and, having first seen that your coffee-pot has been thoroughly cleansed and scalded, put in your ground coffee, with a little white of egg and a crushed egg-shell if it has not been already glazed with egg, and pour over it three pints of fresh, cold spring water. Cover up, excluding every particle of air; and in the morning, about half an hour before breakfast, set the pot on the back part of the stove, and let it come to a boil only just when you are ready to send it to the table.

By this plan of infusion all of the virtue in the coffee seems to be brought out. It is an admirable method. — VIRGINIA COOKERY-BOOK : *Mrs. Mary Stuart Smith. Harper & Brothers, Pubs. (By per.)*

Chocolate.

Scrape fine an ounce (one of the small squares) of Baker's or any other plain chocolate. Add two tablespoonfuls of sugar, and put in a small saucepan with a tablespoonful of hot water. Stir over a hot fire for a minute or two, until it is perfectly smooth and glossy, and then stir it all into a quart of boiling milk, or half milk and half water. Mix thoroughly, and serve at once. If the chocolate is wanted richer, take twice as much chocolate, sugar, and water. Made in this way, chocolate is perfectly smooth, and free from oily particles. If it is allowed to boil after the chocolate is added to the milk, it becomes oily, and loses its fine flavor. — NEW COOK-BOOK : *Miss Maria Parloa. Estes & Lauriat, Pubs. (By per.)*

CHAPTER XVII.

CONFECTIONERY.

CONFECTIONERY.

JESSIE'S BARGAINS.

WHEN Uncle Feodorardo left this world of woes, — which doubtless he looks back upon with a sight that pierces the secret of the storms and showers and sunshine of it, — he left a great gap in it for all the children. What a blessing he was to child-kind, to be sure! And what a peculiar blessing to one mite out of that kind, Jessie by name!

How this little white mite would have kept alive at all, at one time, instead of dissolving back into her elements, if Uncle Feodorardo had not taken her in hand, is one of those dark questions to be worked out with chemical equations. He reminded you, in the process, of those Japanese jugglers who, with their fans, keep butterflies fluttering on the air around them, which, if the fan ceased and they fell to the ground, would be merely the original atoms of torn white paper again. For the changeling was so slight a thing that you could see the sun shine through her hand, and they had threatened to hang her up in the window for a transparency; and she was finally allowed to run wild, in hopes that she might lose her blanched, house-plant look, and get a little of the vigor of the out-door weeds.

It was with this end in view that Uncle Feodorardo, — no uncle of hers, by the by, any more than of all the little people in town, but an exile who had been adopted into every body's heart in the new home, — would entice the flaxen-haired piece of mischief into his garden across the way, and, giving her a little spade, would set her to digging anywhere in the warm brown earth. "She is our mother," said Uncle Feodorardo. "We are made of her dust. When we are peaking, her touch is our best cure." He offered Jessie wages for the work she was to do with her little spade, — wages quite as large as Uncle Feodorardo could afford, for he earned his own livelihood from his garden; and, at any rate, quite the market-value of the work performed, — wages of a penny an hour, and which she was to claim when she could conscientiously say she had delved sixty minutes. Sometimes it took Jessie a whole week before she could honestly earn her penny, for she had a thousand things in that garden to divert her, since Nature and Feodorardo together conspired to keep her active when she could be drinking in health from all the winds that blew about her. . . .

But when at last the penny was hers, no more garden-work, or play either, for that day. It was business, serious business. She hied away with it to the corner grocery; and it was a weary forenoon to the wretched clerk behind the counter there, who must 'have grown to dread the sight of that little figure, if he did not regard its approach as an expiation of his own peccadilloes among the cakes and sweetmeats. Jessie was not like those good children who put their pennies in the missionary-box. She felt, perhaps, that there was a little heathen here at home that wanted the penny; and though she was any thing but starved, yet, except on the rare occasions when she bought a tiny china baby as naked as a pappoose, she always spent that penny for her palate. But stingy with her bargain, — bargain it was always, — a jury of her peers could not have declared her; for though she quarrelled and scuffled with her sisters, in the morning, for the wash-basin or the towels, she always gave them a bit of her macaroon, or her tart, or her plum, in the afternoon, — crying a little bit if they took too big a bite.

She would begin her bargaining by pricing every thing in all the jars deliberately, until at last the half-distracted clerk would cry, "Now you know the price of every thing in this shop, see here! And you can buy, or you can let it alone. The gibraltars are a cent apiece, and so are the barley-sugar sticks, and the apples, and the ginger-snaps. And we don't sell white grapes by the cent's worth, nor guava-jelly. And I sha'n't let you have a quince anyway, because it would give you a colic, and your ma wouldn't like it; and, besides, quinces are two cents this year."

"How much is jujube-paste?" Jessie would ask then, oblivious of the slight to her dignity involved in the reference to colic.

"Well, you can have a stick of that for a cent."

"I don't know as I like jujube-paste," hesitatingly, and climbing higher with her dangerous elbows on the show-case.

"Then what did you ask about it for?" the clerk would say tartly. "We have it in all flavors," he would add, from mere habit. "Then there's Jenny Lind chewing-gum," in a tone half-questioning, half-advising.

"I like real gum better than that," is the reply.

"We're all out of spruce," teetering back and forth on his heels and toes.

"Haven't you any gum-*drops*?" Jessie would ask.

"Oh, yes, plenty of those," snatching at relief.

"How many" —

"Six for a cent," plainly and emphatically.

"I don't think that's quite enough," gently, but full as decidedly.

"Very well. That's the best we can do for you," taking out his pocket-comb now, and soothing his mind by its use.

"Do you ever sell a piece of an apple?"

"Good gracious! I'll *give* you a bite," cries the clerk desperately.

"Oh, no," she answers sweetly; "I don't want you to give me any thing. I'm not begging, I'm buying," grand as a little archduchess.

"Well, then, what will you have?" he demands, leaning over the counter in a state of exhaustion.

"I suppose, though, you don't throw any thing in when people buy?" she asks, slightly modifying her grandeur, as even archduchesses may.

"Not your sort," says this Bayard of the boxes.

"I didn't ask you to throw any thing in," indignantly. "I said I supposed you didn't."

"Come, time's up!" cries her victim as a last resort. "What'll you take? I'm going to close, and go home to dinner."

"I guess, then, I'll take a cocoanut-cake. You said they were " —

"A cent apiece. Yes," with satisfaction at the prospect. And then, as Jessie lays her little hand on the largest one, he is obliged to remark, "But that size is three cents."

Sometimes Jessie withdrew with her cent at this point, outraged and insulted, and made no purchase all that day. But she carried the cent to bed with her; her first thought on waking in the morning was concerning it; her first act was to feel for it; it lay beside her breakfast-plate; and no sooner was she her own mistress again than she returned, bright and early, to her charge, and renewed her haggling. — JESSIE: *Mrs. Harriet Prescott Spofford.* (*By per.*)

Barley Sugar.

One pint of very strong barley-water, strained; two pounds of rock‑candy; lemon-juice to taste. Boil without stirring; then pour into buttered pans, and score into long flat sticks. It is excellent. — THE UNRIVALLED COOK-BOOK. (*By per. Harper & Brothers.*)

Sugar à la Crême.

Take a pound of maple-sugar, put it in a pan, and put the pan into another of boiling water, until it melts into a sirup. Then put in a half-teacupful of cream, and boil for ten minutes. Pour it out into a well-buttered dish; cut it into squares while cooling. *Public Ledger, Philadelphia.* (*By per.*)

Cocoanut Candy.

Equal quantities of white sugar and grated cocoanut; add enough milk of the cocoanut to moisten the sugar, and then put it on the fire to boil, stirring almost constantly. When the candy begins to return to sugar, stir in the cocoanut as quickly as possible, and in a minute or two spread it on dishes to cool, marking it off in squares to cut after it hardens sufficiently. If you would like a portion pink, stir a little pokeberry-jelly into some of the candy while hot, until it has acquired the tint you like. — VIRGINIA COOKERY-BOOK: *Mrs. Mary Stuart Smith. Harper & Brothers, Pubs. (By per.)*

Red or Pink Coloring.

Gather pokeberries just before frost falls; express the juice, and let it drip clear through a flannel or thin muslin bag; to one pint of juice allow three-quarters of a pound of white sugar; boil rapidly together for twenty minutes, and put away in a small glass jar for use. This quantity will last an ordinary family for a whole year, and be found very useful in ornamental cookery. — VIRGINIA COOKERY-BOOK: *Mrs. Mary Stuart Smith. Harper & Brothers, Pubs. (By per.)*

Ginger or Cinnamon Tablet.

"Melt one pound of loaf-sugar or sugar-candy with a little water over the fire, and put in one ounce of pounded ginger or cinnamon, and keep stirring it till it begins to rise into a froth, then pour into a dish which has been first rubbed with a little butter; before it hardens, cut it into the size and shape you approve of for table."

Chocolate Caramels.

Take half a pint of rich milk, and put it to boil in a porcelain kettle; scrape down a square and a half of chocolate, put it into a very clean tin cup, and set it on the top of a stove till it becomes soft. Let the milk boil up twice, then add gradually the chocolate, and stir both over the fire till thoroughly mixed and free from lumps. Stir in half a pint of the best white sugar powdered, and four large tablespoonfuls of molasses. Let the whole boil fast and constantly (so as to bubble), for at least one hour or more, till it is nearly as stiff as mush. When all is done, add a small teaspoonful of essence of vanilla, and transfer the mixture to shallow tin pans slightly greased with very nice sweet oil. Set it on ice, or in a very cool place, and, while yet soft, mark it deeply in squares with a very sharp knife. When quite hard, cut the squares apart. — *Godey's Lady's Book.* (*By per. Pub.*)

Vanilla Toffee.

Put one-quarter of a pound of butter at the bottom of the saucepan, then put in one pound of sugar and two tablespoonfuls of vinegar. Leave it to soak one night. If it looks too dry in the morning, add a little more vinegar. Then put it on the fire, and boil, not stirring it. When you think it likely to be done, stick a knife into the middle of it, and drop it into a cup of cold water, and if it bites crisp it is done. Just before it is done, drop in a teaspoonful of essence of vanilla. Then pour the toffee thinly all over a buttered tin, and it will soon be cold. — *Peterson's Magazine.* (*By per.*)

Stuffed Dates.

Remove the stones from a pound of fine dates (cost ten cents), by cutting them open at one side. Remove the shells and skins from half a pound of almonds (cost ten cents); the skins can easily be rubbed off by first pouring boiling water on the almond kernels; replace the date-stones with the almonds, and arrange the dates neatly on a shallow dish; dust a little powdered sugar over them, and keep them in a cool, dry place till ready to use. The dish will cost twenty-three cents. — TWENTY-FIVE-CENT DINNERS: *Miss Juliet Corson.* (*By per.*)

Creamed Walnuts.

The white of one egg, and an equal amount of cold water, one teaspoonful of lemon or vanilla. Beat until thoroughly mixed; then beat in confectioner's sugar, sifted, until the dough is stiff enough to mould. Break off pieces the size of a nutmeg, roll them till smooth and round. Press the halved walnut-meats on each side, letting the cream show slightly between the meats. One egg will require about a pound and a quarter of sugar. — THE PEERLESS COOK-BOOK: *Mrs. D. A. Lincoln.* (*By per.*)

Walnut Taffy.

Boil half a pint of molasses until it crisps when dropped into water; stir into it one pint of walnut-kernels, and let it cook about ten minutes on a slow fire, stirring constantly. Then put in a quarter of a teaspoonful of soda, stirring it thoroughly in. Pour out into a well-greased pan. — *Miss Lulie Strohm.*

Peanut Candy.

"Boil together one pint of molasses, one gill of brown sugar, and two ounces of butter. When this is growing thick, add one pint of parched and shelled peanuts; then boil the whole fifteen minutes, and pour it into a shallow dish to cool and harden."

CHAPTER XVIII.

COOKERY FOR THE SICK.

COOKERY FOR THE SICK.

Wagtail to Bobtail.—"By the by, Bobtail, I ought to apologize for not having congratulated you on the fortune that you have just stepped into."
Bobtail.—"That my precious Betsy has just stepped into, you mean."
Wagtail.—"True; rather odd, eh?"
Bobtail.—"Odd!"
Wagtail.—"Queer—umph!"
Bobtail.—"Queer—what?"
Wagtail.—"Why, that old Brown, who was no sort of relation to Mrs. Bobtail, should have left the money to *her*, and not to you. Eh, eh?"
Bobtail.—"Not at all odd, Mr. Wagtail; neither is it queer, Mr. Wagtail! *I* never paid Brown any attention: my precious Betsy did. *I* never took him up a basin of broth, or gruel, or arrowroot, in all my life. Now, my precious Betsy was constantly *brothing* him, and *gruelling* him, and *arrow-rooting* him,—consequently Brown, very properly, appreciated her kindness and attentions."—MY PRECIOUS BETSY: *J. M. Morton.*

Mutton Broth.

Boil a piece of mutton until it will fall from the bone; then strain the broth, and let it get cold, so that the fat will rise, which must be taken off; then warm the liquor, and put in a little salt. Swelled rice or barley may be added to it. Veal or chicken broth is made in the same way.—PRESBYTERIAN COOK-BOOK. *Dayton, O. (By per.)*

Beef Tea.

Cut half a pound of lean fresh beef into slices, lay it in a dish, and pour over it a pint of boiling water; cover the dish, and let it stand half an hour by the fire, then just boil it up, pour it off clear, and salt it a very little. — *Godey's Lady's Book*. (*By per. Pub.*)

A Nourishing Omelet.

Dissolve a saltspoon of beef-extract in half a cup of hot water, and stir into it half a cup of the crusts of whole-wheat bread rolled fine. Let them soak over the teakettle while you beat the yolks and whites of two eggs. Stir the soaked crumbs into the yolks, add a dash of salt and pepper, then stir the whites in lightly. Cook in a hot, buttered omelet-pan. Fold, and invert on a hot dish. Garnish with parsley. — THE PEERLESS COOK-BOOK: *Mrs. D. A. Lincoln.* (*By per.*)

Gruel.

"One large tablespoonful of fine Indian or oat meal, mixed smooth with cold water, and a salt-spoon of salt; pour upon this a pint of boiling water, turn into a saucepan, and boil gently for nearly an hour. Stir it frequently, and thin with boiling water if becoming too thick. When done, and cool enough, serve with sugar and a little new milk or cream. Raisins boiled in gruel improve it."

Arrowroot.

Mix a dessert-spoonful of arrowroot with a little cold water; have ready boiling water in a kettle, and pour it upon the arrowroot until it becomes quite clear, keeping it stirred all the time; add a little sugar. When milk may be taken, it is very good made in the same way with milk instead of water, a dessert-spoonful of arrowroot, and half a pint of milk; add a small bit of lemon-peel. — *Arthur's Home Magazine.* (*By per.*)

Ground-Rice Milk.

Boil one spoonful of ground rice, rubbed down smooth, with one pint and a half of milk, a bit of cinnamon, lemon-peel, and nutmeg. Sweeten when nearly done. — *Godey's Lady's Book.* (*By per.*)

Flour Caudle.

Take a large tablespoonful of flour, mix very smoothly with a little milk, and a pinch of salt. Stir it into a quart of boiling milk, stirring it very carefully and thoroughly to prevent burning or becoming "lumpy." Season it with grated nutmeg or a little ground allspice.

(This caudle, or "pap" as country people often call it, is excellent in cases of diarrhœa.)

Panada.

"Six Boston crackers split, two tablespoonfuls of white sugar, a good pinch of salt, and a little nutmeg; enough *boiling* water to cover them well. Pile the crackers in a bowl in layers, scatter the salt and sugar and grated nutmeg among them. Cover with boiling water, and set on the hearth, with a close top over the bowl, for at least one hour. The crackers should be almost clear, and soft as jelly, but not broken. Eat from the bowl, with more sugar sprinkled in if you wish it. If properly made, this panada is very nice."

Milk Toast (for invalids).

Take a couple of slices of bread, and toast well, — that is, crisp. Take new milk or cream, also a bit of butter (varying according to toast required), and melt in a saucepan together. Then dip in the slices of toast, let them soak for a moment or two, lift on to a deep plate, and pour the remains of milk and butter on top. Serve very hot; add salt as required. — *New-York Herald.*

Irish-Moss Blancmange.

Pick over carefully one teacupful of Irish moss; wash it first in saleratus-water, then rinse it several times in fresh; put it in a tin bucket, with one quart of milk; cover closely, and set in a pot of boiling water. Let it stand until the milk begins to thicken, then strain through a fine sieve, and sweeten with powdered sugar; flavor with lemon or vanilla. Wet the mould in cold water, pour in the blancmange, and set in a cool place. When quite firm, loosen the edges from the mould, and turn out on a dish. To be eaten with sugar and cream. — PRESBYTERIAN COOK-BOOK. *Dayton, O.*

Calves'-Foot Jelly.

"Boil four nicely cleaned calves'-feet in three quarts of water, until reduced to one, very slowly; strain, and set away until cold; then take off the fat from the top, and remove the jelly into a stew-pan, avoiding the settlings, and adding half a pound of white powdered sugar, the juice of two lemons, and the whites of two eggs, the latter to make it transparent. Boil all together a few moments, and set away in bowls or glasses; it is excellent in a sick-room."

Egg mulled in Tea or Coffee.

"Beat the yolk of an egg very well, in a tea or coffee cup; stir into it a little milk or cream; then pour on it, stirring it all the time, hot coffee or tea sufficient to fill the cup. If the hot liquid is poured in too hastily, or without stirring it at the time, the egg will curdle, instead of uniting with the tea. Invalids are recommended to try this mixture for breakfast, as being light and nourishing, without being heating."

Raspberry Vinegar.

To four quarts red raspberries, put enough vinegar to cover, and let them stand twenty-four hours; scald and strain it; add a pound of sugar to one pint of juice; boil it twenty minutes, and bottle; it is then ready for use, and will keep years. To one glass of water add a great spoonful. It is much relished by the sick. Very nice. — EVERY-DAY COOK-BOOK: *Miss Neill. Belford, Clarke, & Co. (By per.)*

Apple Water.

"One large juicy pippin, the most finely flavored you can get; three cups of cold water, one quart if the apple is very large. Pare and quarter the apple, but do not core it. Put it on the fire in a tin or porcelain saucepan with the water, and boil, closely covered, until the apple stews to pieces. Strain the liquor *at once*, pressing the apple hard in the cloth. Strain this again through a finer bag, and set away to cool. 'Sweeten with white sugar, and ice for drinking."

Barley Water.

Put a large tablespoonful of well-washed pearl-barley into a pitcher; pour over it boiling water; cover it, and let it remain till cold; then drain off the water, sweeten to taste, and, if liked, add the juice of a lemon, and grated nutmeg. — EVERY-DAY COOK-BOOK: *Miss Neill. Belford, Clarke, & Co., Pubs.*

CHAPTER XIX.

HOME REMEDIES.

HOME REMEDIES.

Herbs, too, she knew, and well of each could speak,
  That in her garden sipped the silvery dew;
Where no vain flower disclosed a gaudy streak;
  But herbs for use, and physic not a few,
Of gray renown, within those borders grew:
  The tufted Basil, pun-provoking Thyme,
Fresh Baum, and Marygold of cheerful hue;
  The lowly Gill, that never dares to climb;
And more I fain would sing, disdaining here to rhyme.

Yet Euphrasy may not be left unsung,
  That gives dim eyes to wander leagues around;
And pungent Radish, biting infant's tongue;
  And Plantain ribbed, that heals the reaper's wound;
And Marjoram sweet, in shepherd's posy found;
  And Lavender, whose spikes of azure bloom
Shall be, erewhile, in arid bundles bound,
  To lurk amidst the labors of her loom,
And crown her kerchiefs clean with mickle rare perfume.

William Shenstone.

Herb Teas.

Pour *one cup* of *boiling water* over *one tablespoonful* of the *herbs*. Cover the bowl, set it over the tea-kettle, and steep ten minutes. Sweeten if desired. *Mullein tea* is good for inflammation of the lungs; *camomile tea*, for sleeplessness; *calamus* and *catnip tea*, for colds and infant's colic; *cinnamon tea*, for hemorrhages; *watermelon-seed* and *pumpkin-seed tea*, for strangury and summer-complaint. A few sprigs of *sage, burnet, balm,* and *sorrel, half a lemon* sliced, and *three pints* of *boiling water*, sweetened to taste, and covered closely until cold, make an agreeable drink for a fever patient. — THE BOSTON COOK-BOOK: *Mrs. D. A. Lincoln. Roberts Brothers, Pubs. (By per.)*

Pennyroyal Tea.

"The virtues of this old-fashioned remedy are vouched for in cholera years, by a correspondent, who says that the pennyroyal herb, made into a tea and drank hot, is the most comforting and active preventive that can be imagined when depressing symptoms set in."

Elder Tea.

"Make a strong tea of *elder-flowers*, either *fresh* or *dried*. Sweeten with honey. This tea is to be drunk as hot as possible, after the person is warm in bed; it produces a strong perspiration, and a slight cold or cough yields to it immediately; but the more stubborn requires two or three repetitions. Used in Russia." This is an excellent remedy for colds attended with feverish symptoms and sore throat.

Slippery-Elm Tea.

Pour *one cup* of *boiling water* upon *one teaspoonful* of *slippery-elm powder* or a piece of the bark. When cool, strain, and flavor with *lemon-juice* and *sugar*. This is soothing in any inflammation of the mucous membrane. — BOSTON COOK-BOOK: *Mrs. D. A. Lincoln. Roberts Brothers, Pubs.*

Flaxseed Lemonade.

Pour *one quart* of *boiling water* over *four tablespoonfuls* of *whole flaxseed*, and steep three hours. Strain

and sweeten to taste, and add the *juice* of *two lemons.*
Add a little more water if the liquid seems too thick.
This is soothing in colds. — BOSTON COOK-BOOK : *Mrs.
D. A. Lincoln. Roberts Brothers, Pubs. (By per.)*

Calamus Candy.

"Two cupfuls of small pieces of sliced root, an eighth of an inch in thickness ; cover with cold water, and boil gradually ; then pour off the water, and add a cup and a half of pulverized white sugar, with water ; simmer long and slowly, stirring frequently ; pour out in buttered pans. In Turkey it is considered preventive of contagion."

> And he felt new life in his sinews shoot,
> As he drank the juice of the calamus-root;
> And now he treads the fatal shore,
> As fresh and vigorous as before.
> THE CULPRIT FAY: *Joseph Rodman Drake.*

Delightful Cough Candy.

Break up a cupful of slippery-elm bark, and let it soak for an hour in water poured over it in the measuring-cup. Half fill a cup with flaxseed, and fill up to the brim with water, leaving it to soak the same time as the slippery-elm. When you are ready to make the candy, put one pound and a half of brown sugar in a stew-pan over the fire ; pour the water from the slippery-elm and flaxseed over it, straining the last, and stir constantly until it boils and begins to turn back to sugar ; then turn it out, and it will break up into crumbly, small pieces. For preachers or teachers who use their voices too much, it will be found an admirable and agreeable medicine, the taste being peculiarly pleasant. It is highly recommended to any one subject to throat affections. The best flavor for it is a little lemon-juice. — VIRGINIA COOKERY-BOOK : *Mrs. Mary Stuart Smith. Harper & Brothers, Pubs. (By per.)*

Excellent Cough Mixture.

Take a handful of hoarhound, boil in a quart of water; add one pint of Orleans molasses, and one pound of brown sugar. Boil to a thin sirup. Put all in a bottle, and add one tablespoonful of tar. Shake while warm, until the tar is cut into small beads. Dose : Take one tablespoonful whenever the cough is troublesome. *Presbyterian Cook-Book, Dayton, O. (By per.)*

Gargle for Sore Throat.

Make a gargle of one teaspoonful of molasses, one of salt, and one half-teaspoonful of cayenne-pepper. Mix these with one teacupful of hot water. When cool, add one quarter of a cup of cider-vinegar. — PRESBYTERIAN COOK-BOOK. *(By per.)*

Salve.

Four ounces of mutton-tallow, two of beeswax, one of rosin, and one-half ounce of gum camphor. Simmer well together; take off the fire, and then add one gill of alcohol. Good for all kinds of sores and wounds. — PRESBYTERIAN COOK-BOOK : *Mrs. W. C.*

Brown Salve.

Two pounds of mutton-tallow, put in as many jimson (Jamestown weed) and plantain leaves as possible; fry until they crimp up, and then strain. To this add about two tablespoonfuls of tar; let it boil up, then pour it into the vessel in which it is to be kept, and let cool. — PRESBYTERIAN COOK-BOOK. (*By per.*)

Balsam Liniment.

"The fruit of the *balsam apple* (*momordica balsamina*) picked when ripe, and preserved in alcohol, is considered very efficacious applied to a fresh wound. Bind a piece upon the wound or cut. In Syria, the fruit is used for the same purpose that it is here; but they cut it open when unripe, and infuse it in sweet oil, exposed to the sun for some days, until the oil has become red. This is dropped upon cotton, and applied."

For a Gathering.

"Soak the leaves of common *dock*-plant in vinegar; apply warm, as often as possible."

Borage.

"This plant contains a certain amount of saltpetre, as may be proved by burning a dried leaf. For this reason, it is used with great benefit for the relief of sore throats. The root is rich in gum, and if boiled yields a mucilaginous emulsion, excellent for irritation of the throat and chest. Very violent attacks of toothache, where the nerve has taken cold, are often cured by holding a portion of the leaves, previously boiled in milk, and applied warm, in the mouth, against the affected tooth."

Thieves' Vinegar.

"Soak two ounces each of rue, sage, rosemary, lavender, and wormwood, for three days in one pint of white-wine vinegar; stand at a short distance from the fire. In each pint of vinegar, dissolve half an ounce of camphor, and strain well. In cases of infection, bathe the nostrils and around the mouth with this preparation. This powerful disinfectant was used during the plague in London, by the thieves who robbed the dead and dying: hence its name."

Scent Sachets. No. 1.

"Take of lavender-flowers, free from stalk, half a pound; dried thyme and mint, each half an ounce; ground cloves and caraways, of each a quarter of an ounce; common salt dried, one ounce. Mix the whole well together, and put into silk or cambric bags. It will perfume the drawers and linen very nicely."

Scent Sachets. No. 2.

"Coriander-seed one ounce, orris-root one ounce, rose-leaves one ounce, mace one drachm, allspice one drachm, lavender-flowers one ounce, sweet-flag (*calamus aromaticus*) one ounce."

ALPHABETICAL INDEX.

	PAGE		PAGE
ALMONDS, salted	208	Beef's Heart, to bake a	52
Ambrosia	205	Beefsteak, French	29
Angel Cake	191	" fried	30
Apple Butter	127	" Pie	31
" Dumplings	165	Beets	106
" Pudding, boiled	164	Biscuit, brown	149
" Sauce, for Goose	66	" drop	151
" " Sunday	166	" egg	150
" Water	227	" Naples	150
Arrowroot	224	" soda	151
Asparagus, to cook	96	" flyaways, or *soufflé*	151
		Blanc-Mange, Irish moss	226
BACHELOR BUTTONS	198	" " raspberry	203
Bacon and Eggs	45	Blackberry Flummery	171
Baked Beans	50	Borage	235
" Custards	169	Bouillabaisse, a Marseilles	
Balsam Liniment	235	receipt for	6
Barley Sugar	217	Bouillon	4
" Water	228	Bow-Knots	199
Bass, boiled	16	Bread	142
Beans, baked	50	" aërated home-made	145
" string	28	" brown	155
Beef *à la Mode*	31	" corn	158
" roast		" French twist	144
" Loaf	33	" salt-rising	146
" Stew or Hash	31	" Vienna	144
" Tea	223	Bride-Cake, rich	199

(237)

Brown Betty............	166
" Bread...........	155
Broth, mutton..........	223
"Bubble and Squeak"...	53
Buns.....	147
" hot cross..........	148
" saffron............	148
CABBAGE, boiled........	103
" red, stewed...	103
" to stew à la cauliflower..	103
Cake angel..............	191
" black.............	196
" bride	199
" cocoanut...........	196
" dried-apple........	195
" gold..............	192
" hickory-nut.......	193
" jelly, fruit.........	196
" marble............	192
" pound.............	193
" silver	192
" sponge, No. 1.......	195
" sponge, No. 2......	195
" twelfth-night......	200
" watermelon.......	193
Cakes, rock.............	187
" oaten............	160
Calamus Candy	233
Calve's-Foot jelly.... .	226
Candied cherries........	209
Candy, calamus.........	233
" cocoanut.........	217
" cough...........	233
" peanut,..........	220
Caramels, chocolate.....	218
Catsup, cucumber.......	117
" grape...........	118
" tomato, No. 1...	117
" tomato, No. 2....	117
Caudle, flour............	225
Celery, to stew..........	105
Charlotte Russe	203
Cheese, cottage.........	90
" Fritters.........	88
Cherries, candied........	209
Chestnut Purée	64
Chicken, a soufflé of......	67
" curry of........	68
" Fricassee of....	67
" jellied.........	69
" Pie............	69
" " with sweet potatoes..............	70
Chocolate...............	212
" Caramels.....	218
" Pudding......	170
Chops, lamb............	39
Chowder, clam..........	24
" lobster........	25
Clam Chowder.....	24

	PAGE		PAGE
Clam Scallops	24	Currants, spiced	118
Clams, hard-shelled, to boil	23	Curry, chicken	68
		" rabbit	77
Cocoanut Candy	217	Custards, baked	169
Codfish Balls	49		
Coffee Cream	206	DATES, stuffed	219
" to boil	211	Dent de Loup Biscuit	197
Cold Slaw, cream dressing for	103	Deer's Head, to cook in camp	75
Coloring, red or pink	218	Dominoes	198
Compote of Gooseberries	171	Doughnuts, editor's	186
Cookies, sour-cream	186	Dried Beef, frizzled	33
Corn, sweet	98	Drop-cakes, hominy	158
" Bread	158	Dumplings, apple	165
" Oysters	98	Duckling Pot Roast	66
Cough mixture, excellent	234		
Cranberries	64	ÉCLAIRS	194
Cream, coffee	206	Eels, fried	21
" Dressing	94	" stewed	21
Creamed Walnuts	220	Egg mulled in Tea or Coffee	227
Croutons	11		
" after dinner	208	Eggs and bacon	45
Croquettes de volaille (Poultry Croquettes)	71	" fricasseed	87
		" frothed	88
		" pickled	115
" Salmon	17	" scrambled	87
Crullers	186	" soft boiled	87
Cucumbers	96	Egg-Plant	107
Cupid's Wells	199	English Christmas Plum Pudding	173
Curds and Cream	89		
Currants, iced	210	" Tapioca Pudding	170

ALPHABETICAL INDEX.

	PAGE
FISH JELLY	20
" scalloped	20
Flapjacks, corn-meal	158
Flaxseed Lemonade	232
Floating Island	204
Flounders, fried	19
Flour Caudle	225
Forcemeat, to make a good	21
French Toast	152
Fricaudeau à l'Oseille	35
Fricassee of Squirrels	77
Fritters, cheese	88
" omelet	87
" parsnep	106
" pork	44
Frosting, plain	202
Frumenty	160
GARGLE for Sore Throat	234
Gateau des Pommes	166
Gathering, for a	235
Gems	145
Giblet Pie	70
Gingerbread, soft	187
Ginger Horse-Cakes	187
Ginger-snaps	187
Goose, to roast a	65
Gooseberries, *compote* of	171
Grape Sherbet	210

	PAGE
Green Peas stewed with Ham and Lettuce	96
Green Turtle Steak (Epicurean)	15
Ground-Rice Milk	225
Grouse, fillet of	78
Gruel	224
Guinea Fowls, roast	71
HALIBUT, fillets of, *à la Poulette*	18
Ham, to boil a	46
" to broil	46
Herb Teas	231
Hominy Drop-Cakes	158
Huckleberry Pudding	172
ICE-CREAM, chocolate	207
" lemon or vanilla	205
" peach	206
" strawberry	206
Iced Currants	210
Indian-Meal Pudding	168
Irish-Moss Blanc-mange	226
JAM, blackberry	128
" crab-apple	129
" gooseberry	128
" raspberry	128
" rhubarb, No. 1	129

ALPHABETICAL INDEX.

	PAGE		PAGE
Jam, rhubarb, No. 2	129	Lobster, chowder	25
" strawberry	127	" sauce	26
Jellied chicken	69		
Jelly, apple	130		
" calve's-foot	226	MACARONI, baked	107
" cider-apple	130	Macaroons	197
" currant	131	Mackerel, broiled	19
" elderberry	131	Maids of Honor	198
" for Cake	196	Mango, pickle	113
" grape	131	Marketing, hints for	54
" of Pig's Feet and Ears	46	Marmalade, pine-apple	129
		Mayonnaise	94
" quince and apple	130	Meat Porcupine	54
" red-haw	132	Melons	96
" strawberry	132	Méringue, rice	167
" Fruit-cake	196	Milk, ground-rice	225
Johnny-Cake	157	Mincemeat without Brandy	185
Jumbles	186		
		Molasses Sauce	173
		Muffins, maize	156
LADY-FINGERS	195	" rye	159
Lamb, breast of, with peas	38	Mush, fried	158
" to roast	39	Mushrooms, fried	93
" Chops	39	" stewed	93
Lamb's Head	53	" pickled	115
Lemon Snow	204	Mustard and Cress	95
Lentils, boiled, plain	99	Mutton, *au Chou*	37
"Left-Overs," utilizing the	63	" Broth	223
		" Steaks	37
"Little Pigs in Blankets"	53	" stewed shoulder of	38
Liver, ragout of	34		

NASTURTIUMS, to pickle. 116	Peanut Candy.......... 220
	Pears, to preserve....... 124
OATEN CAKES.......... 160	Peas, green............. 97
Omelet, a nourishing.... 224	Pettitoes 51
" *au Rhum*........ 85	Piccalilly............... 112
" asparagus....... 86	Pickled Beet Root...... 114
" bread........... 85	" Carrots......... 114
" ham............ 86	" Barberries....... 116
" plain........... 85	" Cucumbers...... 111
" Spanish......... 86	" Eggs............ 115
" *au Sucre*........ 83	" Muskmelon..... 118
" *aux Fines Herbes* 83	" Onions.......... 111
" with jelly....... 84	" Pork, to boil.... 45
" Fritters......... 87	" Mango.......... 113
Onions, baked 105	" Ripe Cucumbers 111
" boiled.......... 105	Pickles, Green Tomato.. 112
Opossums............... 76	" Pears........... 118
Orange Baskets........ . 205	Pie, beefsteak........... 31
" Water Ice....... 210	" chicken............ 69
Oven, to test the........ 144	" custard............ 183
Oysters, broiled......... 23	" cocoanut.......... 183
" Fried to the	" cream............. 183
Queen's Taste. 22	" dried-apple........ 180
" scalloped....... 22	" giblet............. 70
	" green apple........ 180
PANADA............... 225	" lemon, No. 1....... 184
Parsnep Fritters 106	" " " 2....... 184
Partridges, broiled...... 78	" orange, No. 1....... 184
Patties, oyster......... 21	" " " 2....... 184
Peaches, to preserve..... 123	" pigeon............. 71
Peach Leather.......... 123	" prune............. 181

ALPHABETICAL INDEX.

	PAGE
Pie, pumpkin	181
" peach	181
" raisin	185
" rhubarb	180
" squash	182
" tomato	181
" woodcock	78
" crust, flake	179
" Murrey's	179
Pigeon Pie	71
Pig's Feet and Ears, jelly of	46
" Feet Soused	45
Pig, roast	43
Pork, Fritters	44
" salt, with apples	44
" Steaks	44
" Tenderloin on Toast	44
" to boil pickled	45
Potage à la Reine	8
Pot Roast, duckling	66
Potatoes, *au Maitre d'hôtel*	100
" to boil sweet	102
" "Hillocks"	100
" mashed	99
" Saratoga	101
" Scones	101
" Stewed	101
Pot-au-Feu	5

	PAGE
Preserved Barberries	126
" Cherries	124
" Crab-Apple	124
Pudding, amber	169
" chocolate	170
" cup plum	173
" English Christmas plum	173
" English tapioca	170
" Florentine	168
" huckleberry	172
" Indian meal	168
" rice black-cap	167
" Spanish fruit	165
" white or suet	52
" sauce, plain	175
Purée, chestnut	64
" *d'Oseille* (*Purée* of Sorrel)	36
QUINCE CHEESE	126
RABBIT CURRY	77
Radishes	95
Raisins, to stone easily	203
Raspberry Vinegar	227
Red Cabbage, to pickle	114
Rice Black-cap Pudding	167
" Japanese Style	107
" Méringue	167
" Waffles	159

ALPHABETICAL INDEX.

	PAGE
Roast Beef	30
" Goose	65
" Guinea Fowls	71
" Lamb	39
" Pig	43
" Turkey	61
" Wild Ducks	79
Rock cakes	187
Rogrod	167
Roly-Poly	172
Rusk	147
SALAD, chicken, No. 1	68
" " " 2	69
" dandelion	94
" lettuce	95
" potato	102
Sally Lunn	159
Salmon, broiled	17
Salve	234
" brown	234
Sauce, foaming	174
" fruit-syrup	174
" hard	174
" Lobster	26
" molasses	173
" plain pudding	175
Sausages	51
" to keep fresh all the year	52

	PAGE
Scent Sachets, No. 1	236
" " " 2	236
Scones, Scotch	151
Sherbet, grape	210
Shortcake, strawberry	170
Soup, a delicious	10
" celery	9
" corn	10
" eel	6
" mock oyster	7
" noodles for	12
" okra, or gumbo	8
" oyster	7
" pea	9
" rabbit	5
" marrow dumplings for	11
" vermicelli	11
Soused Pig's Feet	45
Spanish Fruit Pudding	165
Spare-Rib	44
Spinach and other greens	93
Sponge Cake	195
Squashes	106
Squirrels, fricassee of	77
Steak, a Spanish	30
" broiled venison	76
" pork	44
Stew, Irish	38
Stock, brown	3
" veal	4

ALPHABETICAL INDEX.

	PAGE
Strawberry Shortcake	170
Sturgeon, roast	16
Succotash	98
Sugar, *à la Crème*	217
" barley	217
Sweetbread, veal	35
TABLET, ginger or cinnamon	218
Taffy, walnut	220
Tea, beef	223
" elder	232
" iced	211
" pennyroyal	232
" herb	231
" slippery-elm	232
" to make	211
Terrapin, stewed	24
Thieves' Vinegar	236
Toast, French	152
" milk (for invalids)	226
Toffee, vanilla	219
Tomato, *au Gratin*	104
" broiled	104
" Preserves	125
" stewed	104
" to preserve	125
Tongue, to boil	34
Tripe, stewed	51
Trout, to fry	15
Turnips, *à la Poulette*	105

	PAGE
Turkey, dressed with Oysters	62
" how to roast a	61
" how to select a	60
Tutti-Frutti	207
Twelfth-Night Cake	200
VEAL and Rice	37
" braised	36
" stewed	36
" Sweetbread	35
Venison Steaks, broiled	76
Vinegar, Thieves'	236
WAFFLES, rice	159
Walnuts, creamed	220
" to pickle	116
" Taffy	220
Water-Cresses	93
" Ice, orange	210
Watermelon Rinds, to preserve	125
Welsh Rarebit	89
Whitefish, fresh, fried	20
Wild Ducks, to roast	79
Woodcock Pie	78
YEAST	140
Yorkshire Pudding with Roast Beef	33

www.ingramcontent.com/pod-product-compliance
Lightning Source LLC
Chambersburg PA
CBHW020802230426
43666CB00007B/810